Tales From The Head's Room

Also available from Continuum

Creating Tomorrow's Schools Today Ken Robinson and Richard Gerver
The Behaviour Guru Tom Bennett
What Makes a Good School Now? David Woods and Tim Brighouse

Tales From The Head's Room

Life in a London Primary School
Mike Kent

Foreword by Gerard Kelly

continuum

Continuum International Publishing Group
The Tower Building, 11 York Road, London SE1 7NX
80 Maiden Lane, Suite 704, New York, NY 10038

www.continuumbooks.com

British Library Cataloguing-in-Publication Data
A catalogue record for this book is available from the British Library.

ISBN: 978-1-4411-8703-1 (Paperback)

Library of Congress Cataloging-in-Publication Data
Kent, Mike, 1943-
Tales from the head's room : life in a London primary school / Mike Kent ;
foreword by Gerard Kelly.
p. cm.
Includes bibliographical references.
ISBN 978-1-4411-8703-1 (alk. paper)
1. School principals--England--London--Anecdotes. 2. Elementary schools--
England--London--Anecdotes. 3. Kent, Mike--Anecdotes. I. Title.
LB2832.4.G7K46 2011
372.12'012--dc22
2010039194

Typeset by Fakenham Prepress Solutions, Fakenham, Norfolk NR21 8NN
Printed and bound in India

For Rachel, who tells me she's very proud of her Dad

Contents

December

January

February

March

April

May

June

July

August

Foreword

There is one thing about Mike Kent's job as headteacher of an inner London primary school that he loves above everything else: the excitement of helping young children learn. And one thing he hates: anything that interferes with that.

Occasionally this is a parent – the ones who think their children can do no wrong, or those who seem to have forgotten why they had children in the first place. Very occasionally it's another teacher or a school leader – especially those who think liking children is a rather eccentric part of the job description.

But what really infuriates Mike are the jobsworths who can measure a school but have no idea how to value it – officials and inspectors who refer to wall-mounted art projects as 'hazardous fire risks', teaching skills as 'person specifications' and children as 'learning outcome units'.

After I became editor of the *Times Educational Supplement* two years ago, Mike agreed to write more frequently for us. His columns now appear weekly in the *TES* and they are incredibly popular. It isn't just his amusing and skilfully aimed kicks at bone-headed educational bureaucrats that make them so attractive. It's also his vivid accounts of teaching: the girl who is thrilled at playing her first tune on the violin; the exuberance of acting in the school play; the unbelievable satisfaction of switching a 'challenging' boy on to learning.

And ultimately that is Mike's greatest talent. He constantly reminds us all – jaded journalists, ambitious politicians, concerned parents and the huge number of people in education who simply enjoy his writing – what teaching is all about, just as we might be in danger of forgetting.

Gerard Kelly, Editor, The *Times Educational Supplement*

Introduction

Ask what a primary school headteacher's job entails, and most people won't have a problem telling you. After all, everyone has experienced the education process during their formative years, and we all have memories of the people who were in charge of the primary schools we attended, even if the memories have become a little faded by the passage of time.

Headteachers, they'll say, are invariably smartly dressed. They have an office of their own and they spend a lot of time in it, because much of their week will be spent talking to parents, receiving visitors, arranging staff meetings, discussing aspects of the school curriculum with school governors, and checking the budget.

They attend plenty of meetings, oversee the curriculum and have the ultimate responsibility for making sure the children in their schools are properly taught. Naturally, they have an important say in who is appointed to the teaching and support staff. And sometimes, if they've got a spare moment or two, they might actually talk to a child.

The reality is rather different. Yes, those are important aspects of the job – some much more so than others – but they run parallel with the side of the job that most people never see.

Last week, I had to repair Nathan's new spectacles for the third day in a row, remonstrate with a parent who thought that her child should be allowed to bring kebab and chips for his packed lunch every day, argue with a pompous fire official who wanted us to remove our colourful staircase work displays, effect a temporary repair on a broken pipe in the kitchen using a spare radiator hose from my classic MG, and attempt to find the little potential plumber who'd skilfully unscrewed a toilet seat and wedged it behind the cistern.

Then there are the many enjoyable things that I choose to do, and which I consider essential components of my job. All of them involve children. I write and produce the Summer Musical, I read regularly to the Nursery children, I run a jazz group, help with the school orchestra, and teach three guitar groups. I take Junior Choir, organize Friday Film Club and arrange our annual Poetry Week. I teach literacy to the older children and have a great time doing science experiments in Assembly. My office door is always open, and children from all over the school come to show me their work.

Then, at the end of the each day, I stand in the corridor and say goodbye to them all. And I know them all by name.

When I was appointed to headship, back in the early eighties, the procedure for becoming a headteacher was very different from today. You'd have been an effective and successful class teacher in several schools, and then you'd apply for promotion to a post of responsibility, which meant organizing and looking after a curriculum area. You'd make sure your local inspector had noticed all your hard work and then you'd apply for a deputy headship.

Provided things went well, headship was only a small step from there. You'd search through the vacancies in the *Times Educational Supplement* and put in some applications. If you were shortlisted, there would be an interview with a local authority inspector, who was knowledgeable about primary education, and then with members of the school's governing body, who often weren't. They'd ask you what you thought about discipline and whether you thought cookery was suitable for boys.

These days, obtaining a headship is not an option to be tackled lightly. There is a National College of School Leadership, and if you're accepted onto its training course – no mean feat in itself – there are lectures to attend, papers to write, scenarios to enact, procedures to be learned and absorbed. Whether, at the end of all this, better headteachers are produced is open to question. Many of the essential skills need to be learned on the job, and it will always be an extremely steep learning curve.

But I've been doing it for 30 years, in an exceptionally challenging area of inner London, and I've loved every minute of it. I can't think of any job that could be more important or enjoyable, and there isn't a week that doesn't bring an infinite variety of balls to juggle, some highly demanding, some very challenging, and many that are extremely amusing.

As you'll discover, when you read this book.

Mike Kent

September

_____

_____

_____

_____

_____

_____

_____

_____

_____

_____

_____

_____

_____

_____

_____

_____

_____

_____

_____

_____

_____

_____

_____

_____

One
Here we go again

September, and the beginning of another school year. My twenty-eighth as a primary school headteacher in an immensely challenging area of inner London. Social problems are legion, the sound of police cars and ambulances forms a constant background, and the challenges of bringing up children in this neighbourhood are tough and uncompromising. People ask me how I've lasted in the job this long. And why. After all, I could have retired several years ago.

But so many things make the job a delight. Certainly, working with a staff of talented, creative people who thoroughly enjoy each other's company reaps enormous rewards. Our school runs like a well oiled machine, and our website is filled with comments from past pupils who say how much they miss us, and how much they now value their primary years.

And it's the children who make the job what it is. I am constantly amazed by their cheerfulness, affection, resilience … and most of all, their humour. It's the humour, especially, that will stay with me long into retirement.

It was apparent from the moment I started teaching, in Islington in the sixties, when the local inspector was testing the metric knowledge of diminutive Freddie, the local fishmonger's son. 'How many centimetres are in half a metre?' he asked, to which Freddie proudly answered 'fifty'. 'Good boy', said the inspector. 'Now how many of these tiny millimetres do you think there are in a metre?' 'Wow', said Fred. 'There must be fucking hundreds!'

Local authority inspectors were eventually replaced in the early nineties by the centrally regulated 'Office For Standards In Education' (Ofsted), and a team of six inspectors would come and visit your school for a week. I was greatly amused by a colleague's tale of a child who'd misbehaved during an inspection and been sent to sit on the threadbare carpet outside the classroom for 30 minutes.

'I assume you've been misbehaving, young man', said a passing inspector. 'We may be able to help. What could your teachers provide that would make school a happier place for you?' The boy looked the inspector firmly in the eye. 'Thicker carpets', he said.

Even as an ancient head, I still teach, and Monday afternoons working on literacy with a less able group from Year 6 certainly had its moments. Asked to write a story that might appeal to Nursery children, Abdul decided upon 'The Magic Chicken' as a title. After scribbling for several minutes, he suddenly appeared fazed. 'How d'you spell bok?' he said. 'Do you mean "book" or "back"?' I asked. 'No, no,' he said impatiently, 'I mean the sound wot a chicken makes … Bok bok bok …'

All schools are allocated a School Improvement Partner, a sort of watered down Ofsted inspector who checks up on the school's progress several times a year, and my new SIP's introduction to our school coincided with Eddie's. Eddie was a highly intelligent eight-year-old, and we'd admitted him without realizing he'd already attended three other schools, all of which, we learned, would have been happy to strangle him.

When he decided he'd behave however he liked on his first morning, I was forced to lead him very firmly out of the classroom to the visitors' chairs outside my office, where he put his feet up and became engrossed in a book. My new SIP arrived shortly afterwards, and she looked sympathetically at Eddie. 'Hello', she said. 'Are you here because you're unwell?' 'Nah,' Eddie replied cheerfully, 'I've just been assaulted by the 'Edteacher.'

But sometimes a child's comment can elevate you for days. Rachel, like Eddie, had also transferred to us from another school, where she'd had a pretty miserable time. After a highly successful year and a starring part in the summer musical, she smiled at me one lunchtime and said 'Mr Kent, I don't want this term to end.' 'Why's that, Rachel?' I asked. 'Because', she said thoughtfully, 'it's been the happiest time of my life.'

After a comment like that, who could say that this job isn't the best in the world?

Two
A dad who hit life's high notes

While hurrying around Sainsbury's to finish my shopping on a chilly September evening I bumped into Theresa. I hadn't seen her since the last of her children left our school, but her husband Tim was rather special ... the sort of dad we'd like all dads to be. Someone who takes his children to interesting places. Someone who reads with them and makes them laugh, or catches them when they leap out of their depth into the swimming pool. He'll be there to catch the tears, too, and he'll swell with quiet pride when they perform in the school concert. He'll do his best through their difficult years ... and then understand, with a little sadness, when it's time to step back and watch them move on and come to terms with their own adulthood.

All three of Tim's children enjoyed school. Even at Reception age, they were often sent to me with an interesting story they'd written, or a little magazine they'd produced at home, or an artefact brought back from a weekend trip. They were keen to write and paint and craft, and their imaginations seemed highly tuned.

Tim was a musician, and his children wanted to play instruments as soon as they came into our Junior department. Tashi chose violin, Molly the keyboard and Lucas guitar and trombone ... because his dad played those. With her effortless enthusiasm, Tashi soon became the most talented violinist we'd had.

Their harmony as a family quickly became apparent. I use the first Assembly of the term to ask the children what they've been doing in the holidays. Many want to come to the front and talk, but Tim's children always had something particularly interesting to say. I remember a seven-year-old Tashi holding the children spellbound on one of these occasions. Her dad had said, 'I've got a good idea. Let's go camping ...', and off the family went in their ancient Volvo to do battle with dreadful weather in a rain-sodden field.

With her effortless command of vocabulary, Tashi re-created the delights of cooking over a fire and eating from rain-filled plates. She'd also had, she added, a wonderful time. And Tim was never happier than when he was close to nature, writing and performing music, or watching the night sky in a field on a clear summer evening.

Under normal circumstances, I wouldn't have seen Tim very often. His children were never a problem. But he was also a very effective school governor, and if he promised to organize anything, you knew it would be done. He had a passionate interest in education and did much musical work with young people. It was hardly surprising he was so loved by his family, and he seemed to have everything going for him.

Which made it all the more devastating when, just before Christmas, he was diagnosed with a virulent form of skin cancer. He wrote to me, saying he might have to stop his work as a governor while he received treatment, but he hoped to be back in the New Year. Another email followed shortly afterwards. He'd had more tests and the odds were against him. He'd been given just three months to live.

His funeral was unlike any other I've attended. The coffin, made from driftwood by his friends, was carried to the crematorium in the trusty old Volvo. His children and friends played their instruments. They sang, and they read poetry. It was involving, uplifting … and utterly heartbreaking.

There can be few things worse than not being there to watch your children grow up. But they'll be fine. Like all great dads, Tim gave them what they needed in their formative years.

And, without a shadow of a doubt, they will look back on their early childhood with untold affection.

Three
Odd body with a kind heart

September brings the first governing body meeting of the school year.

Every school, from the smallest to the largest, has a governing body. This body is made up from a cross section of interested local people ... teachers, business people, parents, retired people who have an interest in education. The governing body meets several times a year, and its role is to be a 'critical friend' of the school, monitoring its effectiveness, making staff appointments, and ensuring its curriculum keeps within the current government's recommended guidelines. That's the theory, anyway. Whether it works or not is somewhat open to question.

I've never been absolutely sure why people want to become school governors. Power? A stepping stone in local politics? Or a genuine interest in how schools work and a passion for making them better? Certainly, governors these days have an awesome and ultimate responsibility for every aspect of school life.

It wasn't always so. When I became a headteacher in the early eighties, a governor's workload was minimal. They simply had to turn up for one meeting a term. Visiting the school wasn't a requirement, so many didn't; and they could be on as many governing bodies as they liked.

In those days, I'd arrive at meetings laden with documents, and listen to earnest but often irrelevant discussions. Usually, a resolution was made for the headteacher to compile even more documentation. Then an experienced colleague gave me a tip. 'Agree to everything, but only do what's important. And anything that doesn't directly affect the children isn't important.'

Back then, most governing bodies had elderly members with kind hearts but meandering minds. Miss Johnson was a shining example. Although petite, she had a ravenous appetite and marked her place at the table with immaculately sliced sandwiches. She'd wait for what she considered to be a tedious item on the agenda, and then tuck in.

Once, she forgot her sandwiches altogether. She'd been for a day at the seaside and returned with a collection of shells that might interest the children. She took a magnifying glass from her bag and spent the next agenda item studying their markings. I was so fascinated, I haven't a clue what the item was about.

Governing bodies often attracted candidates for local politics, who saw them as a good place to practise airing their party views. While discussing the toilets, one of these political hopefuls stated that local people couldn't rear their children properly because they were stuffed into inadequate rooms on crumbling estates. His opposite number volubly defended the council's position. As political immaturity caused both voices to rise, the Premises Officer appeared at the door and asked me if anybody needed to be ejected.

Like juries, governing bodies contain a cross-section of society. This throws up anomalies from time to time. When we co-opted the retired headteacher of an academy for young ladies, she grappled to reach an understanding of life in a tough Camberwell primary. Offering to do a regular slot on Tuesdays, reading 'Beatrix Pottah' to Reception children, she held out for a full half hour, only losing patience when a child scrawled on one of her suede shoes in felt tipped pen. 'What is that?' she snapped. 'I've drawn Peter Rabbit', said the child. After that, her volunteer time was spent digging the school garden.

New governors always start out enthusiastically. When I appointed one recently, she offered to remonstrate with the parents of persistent latecomers. Scanning the front gate video screen in my office, she was astonished to see a parent slip a recently delivered two-litre bottle of staffroom milk under her coat and disappear down the street ...

But, once settled in, governors can also be incredibly supportive. After my first Ofsted inspection, two governors organized a buffet and plenty of wine to celebrate what would undoubtedly be a highly favourable report.

The inspector rose to his feet. 'This', he said with obvious pleasure, 'is a good school!'

Unused to Ofsted-speak, the governors stared at him blankly. 'A good school?' said one. 'We're a *fantastic* school.' The inspector explained that 'fantastic' wasn't part of the inspectorate's lexicon and that 'good' was actually a fine result.

The governors weren't having any of that. They bombarded him with a million reasons why he was selling us short. I realized that it was the first time I'd seen our governors totally united.

Headteachers might find them tiresome occasionally, but oh, the power of a governing body when it's on your side ...

Four
Rispek to Macbeff, innit

Yo doods, lissen up.

I is readin' in dat Time Educashun Supplimint about how some of you is havin' problems with yo learnin' 'cos we teachers ain't speakin' in de language wot you understan'.

Now I don't want you failin' yo tests or de govermint will be leanin' heavily on me shoulder, know wot I'm sayin'? So I hope you is appreciatin' that I has spent my weeken' on a corse run by de local educashun honchos to learn us teechers a bit o' street, innit.

Now, where wos we in our learnin' last week? We was talkin' bout that well-good playright Willyum Shakespears and I was extollin' his virtues. Yo! Wot dat man cood do wiv a feather an' a tub of ink, eh?

Now, we is studyin' Macbeff an' I know some o' you doods is havin' a bit o' trobble unnerstandin' wot this guy Shakespears is on about, but patience man, you gotta give him some respeck. OK, he ain't no Ediff Blyton, but that don't mean he ain't got a tale worth tellin'. I is gonna sum up dis tale for you 'cos I know you is anxious to get outside and do some twiddlin' on yo mobiles.

This honcho Macbeff is a cool dood. He is well in wiv de King, they is like bosom buddies 'cos that General Macbeff am so good wiv a shank he'd clean up somethin' special playin' Grand Theft Auto. People was well feared of him and Bro' Banquo, wot was also a mean fighter.

Anyway, they is returnin' from battle and crossin' this blasted heaf. That ain't Shakespears doin' a bit o' swearin'. You gotta 'preciate that this dood lived in the sixteenf sentry, before you is even born. So Macbeff ain't sayin' 'I hate this blasted heaf, 'tis a bleedin' nuisance', he is sayin' de heaf ain't got much plant growin' on it.

Anyways, they is crossin' de heaf when they is confronted by these three bitches, man, and they is well mingin'. They has warts on their noses and dodgy breff and stuff like dat. They is tellin' Macbeff he will be main man o' Scotland before much time is pass.

Well, when Macbeff's missus hears dis, she ain't waitin' 'round till de King die, so she get her husbind to waste him instead, when they is comin' for tea an' cake one day at their castle. It ain't too long before he is murderin' dat Banquo too.

Nat'rally, Macbeff don't sleep too easy. His missus is up all nite tryin' to wash blood off her hands wot ain't there and sayin' 'Is this a shank I see before me?' And then Banquo come back as a ghost right when Macbeff is eatin' his dinner, scarin' de shit outa him.

Macbeff thinks he better talk wiv them heath bitches again and they tells him 'Beware, man, specially of a dood called McDuffer.' But Macbeff thinks they probly bin on the weed 'cos wot they say don't make a lotta sense, specially when they tell him he can't be wasted by man born o' woman. They tell him to stay cool, man, less he sees Burn 'em Wood come to Duncesname.

So Macbeff don't do no serious frettin', but then McDuffer gets this army o' bruvvers together and they dress up as trees, man, and they come and attack the castle, innit. Macbeff says 'You can't waste me, man, 'cos you is born o' woman'. But dat's the catch, 'cos McDuffer was born in a Caesar Section, so Macbeff is wasted and Malcum de King son get to be main man after all.

Next week, we is doin' Chorcer. Meantimes, text me an essay. Yo!

Five
Leon's change of direction

Leon is six, and knee-high to a grasshopper. He and his angelic smile came into school near the beginning of the school year, accompanied by his mother, asking for a Year 2 place. One of our families had moved out of London recently, and we said we'd take Leon the following Monday.

We never refuse anyone, but we always ring the previous school for background on a new child before his personal file arrives. In that way, we can find out what he's good at, and whether he'll have difficulty settling in. On this occasion, the secretary at the other end of the phone paused, took a deep, ominous breath, and then said 'Hang on. I'll pass you to our special needs co-ordinator ...'

The SENCo couldn't believe her good fortune. 'He's coming to you? Really? Are you sure? What a relief! He's a thoroughly objectionable little boy. His behaviour is appalling, he does no work, he hurts other children, and he hides under tables and spits at staff. I wish you luck. I can assure you that you'll need it ...'

When Leon's file arrived, things looked even more depressing. Police often arrived to turn his home over, and there had been serious involvement with Social Services. We've never excluded a child, but I worried about our chances with this one. Nevertheless, he was going into Susan's class ... and Susan's the sort of teacher who tells you how delightful her class is, but doesn't realize it's because she's so good at her job.

Things went fairly well on day one. Leon was allocated a friend to help him during his first week, and apart from watching the other children cautiously, wandering around the classroom whenever he felt like it, and calling out during lessons occasionally, he seemed like most children we'd taken on. Leon seemed genuinely surprised at how well the class behaved. He obviously wasn't used to this.

The problems started on the second day. Leon arrived at school – very late – looking thoroughly dishevelled, as if he'd just crawled out of bed. He'd been told he had to take the DVDs back to the rental shop before going to school.

He'd had breakfast, a small bar of chocolate, for going to the shop. We gave him fruit and a hot drink, but he was clearly angry.

Later on we discovered he'd had very little sleep: the police had found his baby sister wandering in the street.

At the end of morning playtime, he didn't want to stop playing and he wouldn't line up with his class. He ran off and climbed onto the playtown, hiding in the little house at the top of it. The children went back to their classroom, and a child was sent to fetch me.

'I'm not dragging you inside', I said, when Leon eventually stuck his head through the playtown window and stared at me defiantly. 'If you want to run home, you can. If you want to stay out here, it's up to you, but it's going to rain. And your class is cooking cakes this morning.'

I crossed my fingers and went back inside. Ten minutes later, I found him under a table outside his classroom. 'Do you want to go back in?' I asked. He nodded, and I slipped him back into the room.

By the end of a fortnight, he'd discovered that our school seemed to be a place where you could do lots of interesting things instead of spending the time being told off. He was bright, alert, very talented at art and craft, and, underneath his couldn't-care-less bravado, desperately keen to learn how to read – something that seemed to have been ignored at his previous school.

He quickly formed a strong relationship with Susan. He knew she liked him and he was anxious to please her, even arriving one morning at eight o'clock to see if she needed any help.

In those first weeks, I often popped into his classroom, but he was fine. Now, apart from habitual lateness, which isn't his fault, and the occasional angry outburst, he's settled. But I do wonder what is happening when two schools can perceive a six-year-old child so differently.

Last week, I returned to school after a few days with flu. When Leon saw me, he ran up and hugged me. 'I missed you', he said quietly.

Just three words. But they reminded me, with great force, of how awesome my responsibility as a headteacher is.

October

Six
Once upon a time … no, please listen!

October: the school year is well under way, and on Thursday mornings every week I read to the Nursery children. It's a pleasurable point in my week, because I relished being read to by my teachers and parents when I was very small.

There's a slight problem, though. These days, children aren't read to as much as they used to be. Many parents are too busy, or can't be bothered, and their offspring simply sit in front of a television instead. Listening to a teacher read a story, therefore, can be a shock for the child just starting to experience school life. You're expected to sit still, you can't pick up the remote after three seconds and change channels, you can't talk because it'll disturb other children, and you can't play with something while you're listening. For many small children these days, this is a very steep learning curve.

I always notice this especially in the first two months of the school year. The children aren't absolutely certain what my function is, and now they are suddenly herded together on the carpet and asked to listen to me. I take my coat off and ask who'd like to hold it while I read a story. Hands shoot up. I choose somebody, drop the coat on his head so that he can't see, and the children laugh uncontrollably. Too uncontrollably … I have to use all my skills to get them back into listening mode.

'Here's a great story,' I begin, 'about a caterpillar who was extremely hungry. Let's see what happened to him …' I glance down and notice that Patrick is using his right hand to explore every orifice in his body. Two children move away from him rapidly, and the teacher, ever ready for any eventuality, quickly pulls tissues from a box. Patrick uses them and leaves them on the carpet. Andrea breaks wind, the extraordinary volume of sound out of all proportion to her diminutive size.

'By the light of the silvery moon', I begin. 'Moon', says a voice loudly from the back. 'A little egg lay on a leaf', I continue. 'Leaf', repeats the voice. As I read, the voice repeats, loudly, the last word I read each time I pause. I look up. 'Please sit quietly and listen', I say. 'You'll spoil the story for everyone.'

I continue reading. 'Out of the egg came a small and very hungry caterpillar.' 'VERY hungry caterpillar', says the voice. I plough on, noticing that Jermaine has dropped a playbrick down Tommy's shirt and is anxiously trying to retrieve it. Andrea, meanwhile, has wandered to the home corner, and Billy is yawning loudly. I wonder if I should have retired last year after all.

But as usual, after just a few weeks, there is a dramatic change. My Nursery teacher, already incredibly skilled after just two years of teaching, has moulded the children into a group who can share a story together with immense enjoyment, while appreciating the rules about listening. They now welcome me on Thursdays with huge smiles, and chuckle with anticipation as I take my coat off and ask who wants to look after it.

The sessions still have their amusing moments. As I read 'Fat Cat', who increases in size as he eats people, Emily tells us that her Auntie Doreen looks a bit like that. When I read 'Where The Wild Things Are', Sam says that if we want to see wild, we should see his granny dancing after she's been on the gin. And 'Not Now Bernard' merely provokes the delighted response that they've heard that one loads of times and they recite it to me word for word.

But the loud repeating voice no longer repeats. He often sits in front of the children now, and tells stories. Pretending, apparently, to be me.

Seven
History? Dull it isn't!

I didn't enjoy history at secondary school. It was taught by a tedious gentlemen who made it as dull as ditchwater. And the subject didn't turn me on at training college either. The lecturer who should have fascinated me with the philosophies of educational pioneers even put himself to sleep on hot afternoons, his pen nib slurring down his notepad as he drifted into slumber.

But as a class teacher I found the subject fascinating – probably because I was making up for what I hadn't been taught – and now, as an ancient headteacher, I find myself reading historical accounts of the last century with immense pleasure, probably because I lived through a great chunk of it.

At school, I'm often used as an historical resource. The children listen, astonished, when I tell them that the house I lived in as a child had no electricity, and the bath had a stubby candle on its edge to assist my father when he carried buckets of hot water from the gas-fired copper downstairs. I explain that, in mid-winter, my father often climbed out on the landing to pour hot water over the frozen pipes before we could have a wash.

Of course, there's always the temptation to embroider a story … although Year 6 was only fooled for a moment when I said our house was so cold in the winter that our words came out in chunks of ice and we had to fry 'em in a pan to see what we were talking about.

My passion for history found an outlet in our school museum. I started this shortly after I joined my current school, and over the last two decades we have been given all sorts of interesting artefacts by parents and visitors. Children should be fascinated by the past, and handling real artefacts is a sure incentive for developing that interest.

Amongst our collection we have a bus conductor's rack complete with tickets, magazines from the fifties, a truly massive early video camera, a gas mask, an ancient typewriter, Beethoven's Ninth on a dozen 78rpm records, a 16mm movie camera, an early mobile phone, and a Lott's chemistry set complete with a Bunsen burner for connecting to your mum's gas ring with a bit of rubber tubing. Health and safety officials would have had a field day!

But for me the most fascinating items are the ones that were in everyday use during my first years of headship. The Digitor, for example. This was a clock-shaped early computer, the size of a dinner plate, with a dozen buttons and a small screen. It cost £170 – a fortune at the time – and by pushing a button the user was presented with ten sums. Depending on whether a correct answer was given, either a happy or a sad face appeared. That's all it did, but the children thought it was magical when I demonstrated it in Assembly; and the Digitor's successors, the Sinclair Spectrum and the BBC Microcomputer, were considered technological miracles.

Musical reproduction technology has changed massively, and today's children have difficulty working out how our Dansette record player is used, but they're always amused when I play an early Elvis 78 and explain how horrified my mother was when she first heard it. And when the children show me the amazing animated movies they produce so quickly on their class computers, I show them my four-minute award-winning animated film, made with a Super 8 camera, that took me almost a year to finish!

My museum isn't solely for children, though. Inspectors smile wryly when they see the original National Curriculum. Horrifically expensive, it was changed within months because there simply wasn't time in a school year to teach everything in it.

I wonder if I could find an education minister who'd be willing to sign it …

Eight
Massage the problem? Yes, it is!

No teacher can expect to get through their classroom career without experiencing children who are – to use the fashionable phrase – 'challenging', but I was very amused this month when I read about the novel way a London local education authority was tackling the problem. It spent £90,000 of taxpayers' money on two reflexologists, and their job was to massage the feet of disruptive children.

I couldn't help imagining how this idea was dreamed up ...

Ah, welcome to the meeting, everyone. We thought you might be the ideal people to take this matter forward. Teachers in the borough are fed up with bad behaviour. Children as young as three are swearing at adults, beating up other children, breaking classroom equipment. The education authority is worried, because equipment replacement is expensive. I'm the Senior Education Officer, so I need to get you people devising a solution.

How bad is this behaviour, Barry?

Well, as SEO I don't actually go into any schools, of course. That sort of thing is way down the hierarchical ladder, fortunately. But I can tell you we've sent our schools lots of documentation about getting children on board: personalized learning, deep drilling down, targeting and tracking, hourly assessments for incomes and outcomes, the pupil as stakeholder ...

Isn't this the problem Barry? Year after year, schools are swamped with this stuff. They don't have time ...

Let me stop you there, Deirdre. Valuable though your opinion as a class teacher might be, we do have some important thinkers in the room. Anthony, you're an educational psychologist. What's your view?

Thank you Barry. I think we're all familiar with Gumbert's Occidental Rings and their relevance to patterns of behavioural decline in children? In my view, intensive training courses for teachers on observation of partitional nodes in first category incidence would lead to a steady and sustained improvement at base level.

Thank you Anthony. That certainly gives us something to think about.

Sorry to interrupt, Barry, but I do have some personal experience ...

Everyone in this room does, Deirdre, but as a class teacher you are a mere practitioner. We need to think outside the box. Run suggestions up the flagpole and see who salutes them. Put ideas in the cat's bowl and see if Frisky laps them up ... Anthea, you're a practising school nurse. Any ideas?

Ritalin works well, Barry. Couldn't each school be issued with a weekly Ritalin voucher? Or Mogadon?

Great thinking, Anthea. Perhaps a combination of both would work well. Have to means test it, of course. A school with swearers would receive less than a school with multiple chair throwers. Swearers are more cost effective in terms of broken equipment. The ratepayers would like that. William, you specialize in behaviour therapy. How do you deal with these children?

Well, I don't deal with the actual child, Barry. The LEA employs me to visit classrooms and observe. I make lots of notes, and then advise on ways forward. Unfortunately I've been off sick because a child threw a shoe at me. Would anybody be interested in my book of behavioural strategies? I wrote it on sick leave. I've got copies with me ...

Later, William. Time's getting on and we haven't come up with much. Now, I had an ankle problem last week and the doctor recommended a first-class chap who massaged it and cured it completely. Calmed me down, too. I wondered ...

Massage! Splendid idea, Barry. That'll calm them down! Could we give it a trial first? I've got an ache in my thigh ... could we get Daniel Craig or Jude Law ...

Remember the ratepayers, Anthea. Deirdre, as an Infant teacher, what's your take on this?

You don't need it, Barry. You see, I've discovered something that works. I told a naughty child off yesterday. Firmly. He was quite taken aback. It cost nothing. I'm certain this could be the way forward ...

Oh, that's dreadfully old-fashioned, Deirdre. The ratepayers like to see their councils moving forward. Let's go down the reflexologist route. In fact, I've got an even better idea. Why don't we employ two of 'em ...

Nine
It's the quality, not the ethnicity, that counts

A former adviser on racial problems in schools recently made the extraordinary suggestion that black children might benefit from being educated in 'all black' schools, with black teachers and a specially designed curriculum. It seems to me an appalling idea. The 'expert' thought it would help tackle today's worrying gun culture. I can't for the life of me see how.

This kind of thinking seems to rear its bizarre head fairly regularly. In the late eighties, under a government initiative known as 'Section 11', local authorities were required to recruit ethnic minority teachers to teach children of a similar background who had learning difficulties.

Somewhat naively, it was assumed that such teachers would have a special understanding of these children. It didn't work. The teachers often came from gentler cultures that had immense respect for any form of education, and they couldn't understand – or cope with – the poor behaviour they encountered. Within months, it became almost impossible to recruit suitable teachers.

Sadly, high-profile figures often pass comment without a real understanding of the issues. A leading light in the Commission for Racial Equality once castigated our inner-city Secondaries, saying black boys didn't achieve because the schools were grim and the teachers thoroughly incompetent. He didn't, of course, actually bother to sample a few schools to see what they had to contend with every day.

Neither did he seem to appreciate that many of these children, who came to regard the gangs they belonged to as their families, often came from desperate homes on awful estates. Invariably, a single parent, usually mum, was either struggling to keep her head above water or had simply given up and abnegated responsibility.

When I was first appointed as a headteacher, my school was filled with the children of white, indigenous, working class people. It was never an easy school. Camberwell was, and is, an area of exceptional deprivation. But gradually, over the years, the population of my school has changed completely. A high proportion of the children are now from black and ethnic minority families. Frankly, I've hardly noticed. Children are children … unique, and endlessly interesting.

What hasn't changed, though, are the expectations of their parents. With few exceptions, they want the best possible start in life for their children. They want them to be happy and settled, they want school to be stimulating and exciting, and they want their offspring to be able to read and write and add up. They have a right to expect all these things, and so have their children.

Our parents couldn't care less whether their children are taught by black or white teachers, as long as the teaching is of a high quality, and no black parents have ever told me they'd like an 'alternative curriculum', whatever that means.

All our inspection reports have commented positively on the racial harmony within our school, and this undoubtedly emanates from the staff and their interaction with parents and children. The teachers like each other, they get on well, they are enormously talented, and they thoroughly enjoy the children they teach. The children, quite simply, sense this and respond to it. As children do, black or white.

In my second year of headship, I appointed an outstanding class teacher as my deputy. She was wonderful to work with. She was also black, and undoubtedly this made for the ideal combination – an ethnically balanced leadership team. Two years ago, she retired, and given the ethnic nature of our school now, it would have been helpful to have another black teacher to replace her. However, the teacher we appointed was white, because we felt she was the best candidate for the job.

And this, surely, should always be the ultimate criterion.

Ten
Working wonders. With glue

As a headteacher in these enlightened times, I'm expected to spend a great deal of my time studying graphs, charts and data, in order to 'drive up educational standards' in my school. Politicians seem to see schools as businesses these days, and children as tins of beans on a sales chart.

In fact, of course, the real delights of my job revolve around children and people. And fixing things. In school I've acquired a reputation for being a Mr Fixit, and there are certainly always plenty of things to fix.

Like the toys that regularly come up from the Nursery class, after a child has accidentally fallen over it, or on it, or dropped it, or experimented by separating the toy into its component parts just to see what makes the wheels go round.

Or Nathan's spectacles. Since joining us at three-and-a-half, Nathan has had problems with his specs and, as a wearer myself, I sympathized from the start. While he was in the Nursery class, Nathan's heavy plastic frames slid down and off his nose as soon as he involved himself with anything more demanding than sitting still. I cured this with a small blob of Blu-Tack carefully wedged between the ridge of his nose and the bridge of the frame, and he was fine as long as he moved around carefully.

The real problems came when he moved to the Infants and acquired metal frames. Nathan would hurry into my room after a boisterous playtime, clutching spectacles that were distorted into unbelievable shapes. A lens would have fallen out, a frame arm would have twisted, or fallen off ... or they would be completely broken into their constituent components. But Nathan had absolute faith in my ability to open a drawer, find my box of miniature screwdrivers and repair his specs, even if he walked out of my room sporting a faceful of masking tape.

My teachers often need a bit of help, too. When one of our Reception teachers stood looking despondently at her car, which wouldn't start, I offered to have a look. I'm a classic car enthusiast, though, so I didn't think I'd be a great deal of help on her modern

Vauxhall, but corrosion had built up on the battery terminals and they simply needed cleaning. She looked astonished when the car started immediately. Assuming I could probably fix anything, she sent me the kitchen play units she'd bought for her classroom home corner. She'd tried to assemble them, and despaired.

Attempting to put these together made an IKEA wardrobe look like a child's jigsaw puzzle. I struggled for several hours, until I realized I'd put the units together back to front and upside down. I got there in the end, but I don't think an inspector would have believed what I'd been doing all day.

The school kitchen certainly benefited from my interest in old cars though. One morning before school, I found the Cook on her hands and knees. The bottom section of a pipe under the sink had broken, our Premises Officer was away, and there was a rapidly growing puddle of dirty water on the floor. I hunted in the boot of my car, found an old MG radiator hose, and fixed it to the bottom of the pipe with a jubilee clip. I ate well that lunchtime.

Glue – of varying strengths – is an essential commodity in my Mr Fixit kit. Few weeks pass without jewellery or a broken toy needing a blob. Andrea's shoes needed more than a blob, though. After a strenuous game of lunchtime football she presented me with a shoe in four pieces. Could I please put it back together, otherwise she'd be in trouble at home. The job demanded my strongest glue, delicately hammered panel pins, sandpaper and some rubbing compound. She was extremely impressed with my repair.

So much so that she arrived the following morning with a shopping bag, which she dropped on my desk. 'My Nan thinks you're really clever', she said. 'Can you do the same thing with the two pairs she's put in the bag?'

Eleven
Pitched battles – and that's just the parents

It's still fairly early in the term, and I chat to the parents as they take their children to and from school.

Since I've been here for many years, I know most of them well. Virtually all our parents are friendly, supportive and interested in their children's education, but since our school is in such a challenging city environment I always have to be prepared for the determined troublemaker, since aggression can explode at a moment's notice and quickly get out of hand.

I discovered this during the exceptionally steep learning curve of my first year as headteacher. On the opening night of a musical show that I'd written, we were less than 15 minutes into the action when I noticed a commotion on the other side of the hall. A mother had accused a woman in the next row of sleeping with her husband. She'd obviously come with the intention of accosting her and was well oiled with lager.

In seconds, a scuffle had broken out, and while the children valiantly carried on acting, a tall, newly qualified male teacher, who happened to be nearest to them, bundled the pair into the corridor and down the stairs, receiving a knee in the groin for his trouble. On stage, my little actors hardly skipped a beat, but I wondered whether it might be worth breathalysing the audience before the next performance.

I'm always amazed how involved some parents become in their offspring's petty squabbles. One Monday morning, Jasmine's mother followed the class into the corridor and pushed Andrea's mum forcibly, saying that Andrea had stolen Jasmine's coloured pencils and she wanted them back, right now. Andrea's mum, no stranger to confrontation, snorted angrily in denial. Fortunately, the teacher had got her class safely inside the classroom, distracting them by reading a story very loudly.

In the corridor, the two parents began shoving each other, and minutes later they were tussling on the corridor floor, at which point the Cook – a local stalwart just as big as they were – strode out of the kitchen and threatened to pour cold water over the pair of them. By the time I got downstairs, both parents were leaning sheepishly against the wall, breathing heavily and apologizing profusely.

Serious arguments between parents are rare, but if they're going to happen it'll usually be in the playground, often when the weather is very hot. One July afternoon, just before hometime, a woman strode into the playground and accused a much smaller mother of shouting at her daughter. A row broke out, and what the smaller mother lacked in stature she certainly made up for in strength, ripping the large woman's blouse off and revealing her ample bosom to an astonished group of Year 6 boys as they were coming out of school.

Before long, the women were surrounded by intrigued children, a Premises Officer who didn't dare get between them to pull them apart, a dozen mothers trying to calm things down – and me. Fortunately, the larger woman's boyfriend suddenly drove up and she ran off to join him.

But the most spectacular incident of my career occurred during an after-school meeting with Social Services and a family suffering horrendous problems. Five minutes into the meeting, mum decided she'd had enough and began shouting abuse. Shoving her chair backwards, she stormed into the corridor and kicked over the SENCo's heavy filing cabinet.

At this point, the father turned up fuelled by illegal substances, and began a pitched battle with the mother and her eldest son. The door flew open as they rolled against it, and they collapsed in a heap on the corridor floor, staggering to their feet only to pick up some metal music stands to chase each other round the room with. I felt as if every serious parental incident in my career had been mere preparation for this one.

The real downside was that the filing cabinet contained twelve bottles of first class wine on special offer that the SENCo had been meaning to take home that evening ...

Twelve
Discipline is deadly serious

Another teenager stabbed to death. In a crowded tube station this time. Rival gangs, many of them in school uniform.

It's what all parents dread most, and we do everything possible to shield our children. We run them to school, ring their friends if they're later home than they'd promised, ensure they carry their mobiles so that we can locate them. We remember the freedom of our own youth and we wonder how on earth things could possibly have come to this.

In reality, we know. Feckless fathers siring youngsters and casually moving on; bored teenagers seeking increasingly extreme highs; parents and teachers unable to control poor behaviour; the disappearance of the extended family; children constantly aware of their 'rights'; a materialistic and manipulative society; easy access to questionable media material. I could spend the rest of this page giving reasons – but you know them already.

Usually, after the latest outburst of teenage public disorder, schools are targeted. We must do more to counter racism. Or bullying. Or aggressive behaviour. Or teaching standards. But we won't even have approached the heart of the matter – which is that we're frightened to discipline our children these days. If we do, we're likely to have social workers knocking on our doors.

I've got policy documents coming out of my ears. Schools have to write one for everything. If your anti-bullying policy is the size of a telephone directory, then fine, you're doing something. If it isn't, it proves you haven't a clue. We're told that bullying and poor discipline are endemic, and we read about uncontrollable six-year-olds shouting obscenities and kicking teachers. Schools are required to deal with an unruly child by consulting a policy, because 'following procedure' avoids trouble from parents and the local education authority.

This takes time, during which the child actually becomes more unruly. Eventually, when nothing has changed, everybody sighs with relief because the child is excluded, goes off to secondary school, or the family relocates. It certainly can't be called problem solving.

Ours is a happy, settled school in the toughest of areas. It's taken years to achieve, we still work hard at it every day, and we certainly have our hairy moments. But the children are constantly reminded of one simple rule: in a civilized, safe school there's room for plenty of individuality, but not at the expense of others. If teachers experience difficulty with children, I'm available, and I will chastise a child, however young, in no uncertain terms. I know I'm not seen as an ogre, but the buck stops with me.

We don't spend hours listening to Damien explaining in great detail why he felt it necessary to thump Charlie, we don't give good behaviour certificates, we don't offer 'anger management' or make contracts with children. They are *expected* to behave ... and, like all children, they respond to a secure, highly enjoyable environment with exceptionally clear boundaries.

We've written a behaviour policy, because we were required to, but nobody ever reads it. You can feel our policy when you walk into the school. Children and teachers smile at you warmly. If students on teaching practice ask for my discipline policy, I tell them to come back in a week – because by then they'll understand what our 'policy' is without needing to read a thing.

Primary school years are so important. We need children to become responsible social creatures right from the start. And we have to insist that parents back us up, taking full responsibility for their children too. Yes, more parents need to work these days, but the proliferation of breakfast clubs and after hours clubs allows parents to offload some of that responsibility very easily. Why bother to have children if you don't want to enjoy as much time with them as you can?

Between us, if we can't succeed before the child goes to secondary school, it'll already be too late.

November

Thirteen
Suspicious happenings in Henry's house

It's November, and Year 3's first educational outing of the year.

Listening to my teachers recounting their traumas on what should have been a straightforward trip to Hampton Court Palace, my mind skips to the teaching days of my youth. Going on a visit was never a big issue. No risk assessments, one teacher to every 500 children, and on a School Journey you could tell them to go and explore ... and to be back by six o'clock if they didn't want to miss their tea.

These days, if Charlie missed his tea, Mrs Brown would probably sue. Then there's the medicines; have we got all the asthma pumps? The creams? No plasters, of course ... health and safety rules. And should we take Raymond? You know what he's like. What if he suddenly goes berserk? Though if we don't take him, we'll probably contravene his human rights ...

Transport is an issue. Coaches are fine: the children are strapped in, and sick bags are to hand. Buses are okay, if you can keep everybody together on the top deck. But trains are something else, as my young teachers discover. Watch the platform gaps like a hawk, make sure your little treasures don't cause the general public to flee the carriage, and be certain no children are left on the train. My teachers manage all this successfully, only realizing after a headcount on arrival that Billy and Ephram, absorbed in the contents of each other's packed lunch bags, have already headed out of the station by an exit in the opposite direction.

But take a deep breath, and on to survey the armoury on the Palace's entrance hall walls – where Gregory points out that his brother has some stuff like that – before meeting the guide who will escort them through the palace rooms.

'Who knows King Henry's surname?' she asks brightly. 'Easy!' shouts Thomas, 'It's "Eighth".' Aisha says no, she thinks it's something to do with chewing, and Harry eventually calls out 'Chewder'. 'Correct!' says the guide. The children punch the air proudly and hurry eagerly into the first bedroom – far too eagerly, as Kevin doesn't notice the rope protecting the four-poster bed and sets off a piercing alarm.

Attendants run in, muttering about teachers who can't be bothered to keep children under control these days. The guide implores the children to look carefully and not touch ... well, anything ... and the group is ushered rapidly along the corridor to another, larger, bedroom.

All stays relatively calm until the group enters the Tudor kitchen, where Sadie slips on the stone floor and bumps into Darren, who falls against the stand supporting a huge soup tureen. It was, said one of the teachers, like watching your life pass before you in slow motion as the thing crashed to the ground. 'Good thing you're not living in Tudor times', says the guide to Darren. 'They'd have had your head off for that!'

Once the children are back on the train, my teachers breathe a sigh of relief. What could possibly happen now? And then what used to be called a Gentleman Of The Road, well past the alcoholic point of no return, steps into the carriage.

He accepts David's offer of a crumpled tuna sandwich, and proffers a swig from his beer bottle in return. 'Are you their teachers?' he grins at my staff. 'Well, I reckon you're much too young. Ain't they too young, kids?'

Three stops further on, when three cans of lager and a tobacco rolling machine have made an unexpected appearance from a grubby coat pocket and my teachers feel the offer of them being handed around is imminent, they ask the platform attendant to intervene. 'Oh, it's only Bob', the attendant says, peering into the carriage. 'Bob always rides this train in the afternoons.'

There's a visit to the Tower of London available soon, but my Year 3 teachers are kindly offering it to Year 4 instead ...

Fourteen
A close shave with a piano lid

Primary school children love music. In my opinion it's vital to the curriculum, and the children at my school are particularly lucky.

We have three choirs, a full school orchestra, and plenty of other instruments such as guitars, keyboards, recorders and masses of percussion. Peripatetic teachers visit each week to supplement all the music going on, and their task is to raise our best instrumentalists to school orchestra standard. They're always thrilled that our children should be so enthusiastic about music.

It's certainly light years away from the music teaching I experienced at the start of my career in the sixties. In the first school I taught at, there was hardly any music at all, but Mr Morris visited twice a week, taking classes for half-hour singing lessons. The children would troop into the music room, basically a disused classroom with an ancient piano in one corner and piles of lost property in the others, and sit down in front of him.

He had to turn his back on the children to play, and since the songs he chose were unbelievably tedious, the children fooled about, singing too loudly or deliberately out of tune. When they tired of that, they'd dig through the lost property and throw things at each other as soon as Mr Morris wasn't looking. Invariably, when I collected my class, some children would be crying because the throwing had progressed from rolled up socks to old shoes. Very soon, I was taking my guitar into school and doing my own music lessons.

Miss Jameson, at my next school, was also a visiting teacher. Although highly accomplished – she played piano, recorder and flute – she was an exceptionally nervous lady and I felt she'd have been more comfortable in a small private school. She was also extremely shortsighted, and couldn't cope with teaching the recorder to more than six children at a time. After six months, the honking noises the children produced hadn't changed much, but Miss Jameson was such a kindly lady that the head hadn't the heart to move her on.

Her eyesight problem proved a real hazard in the staffroom, though. Once, I inadvertently put my plate with a breaktime doughnut on the floor while I talked to a colleague. When I turned back, the plate was intact but the doughnut had vanished. Then I realized Miss Jameson had walked across the room and was now standing at the notice board, my doughnut neatly impaled on one of her high-heeled shoes.

But for sheer eccentricity, Miss Bakewell in my third school beat them all. She was appointed to teach recorder to the juniors and play the piano in Assembly, and when seated at the piano her eyes glazed and she became totally at one with her instrument. Ashkenazy would have given her a sticker for style and concentration.

School concerts were her forte, and on those occasions she rose magnificently to the challenge, dressing for the occasion and embroidering whatever songs the children were singing with a lengthy introduction and a dexterous display of fingerwork. The children stared, fascinated, as she swayed in time to her playing, hammering the keys formidably as she reached musical climaxes. All except Mark.

Mark was not only small, he was also very naughty, and he didn't relish having to sit still during formal events. During one Christmas concert he'd been manoeuvred by his teacher into a position under the piano keyboard, where it was thought he couldn't fiddle with anything. Miss Bakewell reached a thunderous crescendo and lifted her hands exultantly from the keyboard ... just in time to see a small hand appear over the black notes and whack an F sharp. For a moment, Miss Bakewell was stunned. Then, infuriated, she slammed the lid of her piano down with a mighty bang.

How she missed severing Mark's fingers I'll never know. But in future music lessons, it was very noticeable that children kept a respectful distance between themselves and Miss Bakewell's piano ...

Fifteen
The perils of the PlayStation

You wanted to see me, headmaster?

Ah, come in, Mrs Smith. Thank you for bringing Tommy along with you. I just wanted to mention that we're sending him to the school allotment next Tuesday.

That's fine. His class goes there for an hour sometimes …

I know. But the thing is, we're sending him there for three days. With some children who are … um … similar to Tommy.

Sorry, headmaster, I don't understand …

Would you both sit down in my comfy chairs? Now, Mrs Smith, watch closely as Tommy lowers himself onto the cushion. What did you notice?

He travelled quite a long way down, headmaster.

He certainly did. And that's because he's a very large lad. A very large lad indeed. I'm afraid he's what we call obese. And that's a shame, because our teachers spend lots of time talking to their classes about healthy lifestyles and eating the right kinds of food.

Oh, he knows all about that, headmaster. You ask him anything about food, and he knows exactly what he should eat.

So he makes sensible choices at home for his meals?

Oh, I wouldn't say that. But he always thinks about sensible choices. It's just that he prefers kebab and chips.

Well, everything's fine in moderation, of course. But he needs to balance his eating with fruit, salad and vegetables as well. And exercise, of course.

I know. I've told him that. But you can't tell your kids anything these days, can you?

The trouble is, Mrs Smith, there's an unfortunate knock-on problem for the school. We have quite a few children like Tommy who are overweight, and now Ofsted has got involved. You've heard of Ofsted, haven't you? They're visiting next week.

They're the people who come into schools and frighten teachers, aren't they?

That's right. They'll be checking up on overweight children, and blaming us if we've got too many, you see. Our inspection report could suffer as a result. If we become a failing school, my mortgage could be on the line.

But I thought Ofsted inspectors came to see if children are making good progress with their lessons?

Ah, that's what used to happen, when the government had oodles of money for five-day inspections. Things are leaner now.

But hasn't the government said that standards in schools are rising?

It has, and they are. But that's the problem, you see. If standards keep on rising there won't be much need for a mighty government organization like Ofsted.

And inspectors would have to be laid off?

Exactly. Thousands of 'em. They might even – and I can see them quaking in their boots at the thought – have to return to the classroom. After all, the world of education is littered with dubious and expensive consultants, so they won't find much work in that direction ...

So they've decided to inspect overweight children like my Tommy, as well as educational standards?

Correct, Mrs Smith. The more things they can inspect, you see, the easier it is to persuade the government not to disband them.

So it's the school's fault if children are fat?

Yes. And bored. You see, they're also blaming us if children are bored in class. Which brings me to the next point. Tommy's class teacher spends hours making her lessons creative and exciting, but Tommy keeps falling asleep.

It's because he's on his PlayStation till late. I tell him to turn it off, but as soon as I go out of the room he turns it back on again.

Can't you take the thing out of his bedroom?

He'd never forgive me, headmaster. It wouldn't be worth the aggro.

And that's why we're sending him to the allotment, Mrs Smith. Killing several birds with one stone, as it were. Tommy can do some energetic digging and vegetable growing.

He won't like that, headmaster. He's not very keen on exercise.

No, but at least he'll be out of the way until Ofsted's moved on ...

Sixteen
Hit and miss is par for the course

'Continuing Professional Development.'

It sounds rather grand doesn't it? When I was a class teacher, it was called 'Going On A Course'. And 'Learning differentiation for positive outcome'? Well, that was called 'Charlie won't be able to do the hard stuff, so make sure you give him something a bit easier.'

But although education contains far too much jargon these days, CPD is actually very important. Teachers need to keep in touch with what's happening in education, if only to challenge some of the zanier philosophies, and my staff often come back from courses with good, useful ideas.

Certainly, I think the quality of courses has improved enormously, but there's always the exception. I remember attending a turgid sessions on primary school strategies for maths and literacy which made me want to take my own life, although a course on 'safer recruitment' was fascinating – if only because I hadn't realized there are 28 defined stages in the process of appointing teachers. And that's before you get them checked out for any dubious past activity by the Criminal Records Bureau.

Just fancy: all this time, I'd been appointing teachers because they showed passion about education, related well to children, and had bright, lively personalities. Silly me.

Because I've been in primary education for most of my life, I can remember attending some highly questionable courses, including a three-day affair usefully titled 'Raising literacy standards in your classroom; a hands-on practical guide'.

Hands-on it certainly was. On day one we were split into groups, given copies of a famous poem, and told we had two hours to dramatize it. Then each group entertained the others. On day two, the groups were given a portable tape recorder and dispatched to the local woods. Our mission was to record the sounds of nature and write a short play with sound effects. To entertain each other. On day three, everybody had to write a short autobiography, and then read them out to entertain ... well, you get the idea.

As I caught the train home, I realized the consultant had earned his generous fee for doing virtually nothing. The activities were basic things we'd do with children anyway, and we'd learned little that would raise the standards of literacy in our classrooms.

Sometimes, aspects of professional development were simply bizarre. During the nineties, you wouldn't be hard pressed to find two-day courses on BAT training. Not the creatures that emit a loud squeak, you understand (although I suspect much squeaking was done about the quality of the courses), but Behaviour Attitude Training. The idea was that some children behaved badly in class because communication between teacher and child was too negative.

Well, that's not an unlikely premise, but teachers attending the course were shocked to find the suited gentleman leading it – who, incidentally, had never been a teacher – accusing them of being negative virtually all of the time. Teachers, he'd say, simply didn't realize just how negative they were.

To prove it, he handed out click counters, like the things you attach to the spokes of your bicycle wheels, so that everybody could go away and record how many negative things they said in one week. When the group reconvened, results were shared, graphs drawn, assumptions made ... and a BAT certificate awarded.

But sometimes, a course leader did work incredibly hard. As a young teacher, I attended a three-day maths event. From 8.30 a.m. on the first day to 6.00 p.m. on the final one, we experimented with every mathematical concept that should be explored in a primary classroom and we had a wonderful time. On the second day, a teacher gently mentioned that it was lunchtime, only to hear our dedicated and charismatic leader say 'Oh, let's just carry on for a bit. There's so much we haven't done yet.' Eventually, she gave us just enough time to grab a sandwich, but we didn't mind, as we'd gathered enough exciting material for an entire term.

And that's what I call real professional development.

Seventeen
Pussyfooting won't help naughty boys

Recently, I opened my newspaper to find an education minister telling us how much behaviour in our schools has improved.

It came as a surprise to me. Especially after watching a Channel 4 TV programme the same evening about badly behaved primary-school children. The statistics were staggering; the programme makers had carried out a massive survey of primary teachers and no less than 93 per cent of them had said they'd experienced very disruptive behaviour in their classrooms during the last eighteen months.

The programme became more jaw-dropping by the minute. We were taken to a special primary unit where three adults – yes, three – were shown restraining a child and carrying him to a room where he could calm down. The room, like a large prison cell, was totally devoid of any furniture or equipment, just in case the children escorted there kicked it to pieces.

As the child was carried, he made the appropriate gestures of struggling to get away and telling his captors to fuck off. Then he stood kicking the door while being told it would be helpful if he made some 'sensible choices' about his behaviour. The programme concluded by stating that aggressive behaviour like this could be avoided if there was funding for 'nurture groups' in schools.

When children are extremely disruptive, the reason is usually obvious. One child in the programme, for example, had a mother with a drink problem. Another came from a chaotic home. And yet here were teachers asking children who'd experienced virtually no sense of normality to make 'sensible choices'. Watching the programme, it struck me that, in every example we saw, the child was in charge. At no time did an adult challenge the poor behaviour. It was all about the child's options and 'choices'.

When I became a headteacher, the behaviour of my top juniors was grim. I needed to sort it out, because younger children look up to the older ones, so I spent every Tuesday teaching Year 6. They had individual desks in those days, and on the first Tuesday they banged their desk lids continually, watched my reaction to see what

I would do about it. I was the headteacher, and if I couldn't crack it, we'd had it.

I'd been expecting something like this, so I put on a theatrical display of extreme disappointment and anger. They certainly sat up and took notice. From that moment on, I didn't give them an inch. And, gradually, they discovered that my lessons were entertaining and that I might be worth listening to.

Those days are long gone, but the principles are the same. There are two essentials for good behaviour in primary schools: high quality, caring teachers, and exceptionally clear behaviour boundaries, adhered to by everybody. The primary years should be interesting and exciting, but children need to know where they stand. Especially potentially disruptive children who need kind but decisive adults to set the boundaries for them, not pussyfoot around them.

Good behaviour starts in the very early years, and I am extremely firm with small children who can't behave. They, too, are astute enough to test the water in order to see what you'll accept. If you don't get things right when children are very small, you haven't much of a chance later on.

At my school, the biggest difficulties occur with children transferring to us from schools that tolerate poor levels of behaviour, excuse it with a fancy psychological label, or don't do anything about it until it's become a real problem. We always deal with it successfully, but it's only a small step from there to the behaviour shown in the TV programme. The vision of three adults carting a small child off down the corridor will stay with me for years.

God forbid that I should ever need to do that.

Eighteen
It's the beautiful game. Just make sure you win

Okay team, gather round me on the bench. I want to talk to you all about next week's football match against St Gripewater's.

Now, you don't need me to tell you that playing the beautiful game is the most important thing in the world. After all, what is life all about? Yes, earning fabulous amounts of money. You may only be at primary school now, but if you can score goals, and get yourself talent-spotted, one day you too could be up with the greats, earning thousands of pounds every second, opening a string of nightclubs, and having a lot of fun with the ladies.

But make no mistake about it, the most important thing is winning, and that's what we're going to do next week when we play St Gripewater's. We're going to make them lose their nerve, and then we're going to beat them into the ground. We want them walking off the pitch with tears streaming down their faces. They're a bunch of losers, and we're going to prove it to them. Now, I've shown you video clips from professional games, and you've watched all the important matches in the World Cup, so you're already familiar with some of the things I'm going to tell you; but pay close attention.

What is the referee for? Damien? Yes, partly right, he's there to make sure the game is played fairly, but remember, he's only giving one man's view. Next week's game will be refereed by their deputy head, Mr Jellyleg, and he's a bit past it, so disagree with him if he blows the whistle against you. In fact, if you hassle him a bit, it's quite likely he'll think twice about cautioning you again. Get up close to him and shout in his face, like they do on the television. It helps if you wave your arms about a lot, too.

Remember, we don't like St Gripewater's. Scowl at them, make them feel miserable. You might want to give one or two of their players an aggressive shove as well, but don't do it when the referee is looking, or you might get sent off. Of course, you can always argue about that as well, but if you do get sent off, swear a lot and chuck your boots around. With a bit of luck, you might even hit one of the Gripewater reserves.

Now, it's quite possible that you'll kick the ball over the sidelines occasionally and the linesman will wave his little flag at you, but that doesn't mean you have to take any notice. In fact, it's worth arguing with him too, because he'll probably be mistaken. After all, this match isn't going to be on television, is it, so get away with everything you can.

Now, a bit about gobbing. Look at any close-up in a match on television, and you'll see the professionals gob on the grass. It's the macho thing to do, but be a little careful. Some of you can gob a good couple of metres now, but you need to make sure you don't hit one of your own players. Of course, if you happen to hit a player from St Gripewater's, that's not a problem.

Your toughest challenge will be Crusher Johnson. Go for him in the early part of the game. Two or three of you should try to trip him up and then accidentally jump on his right leg. When he starts howling and rolls around on the ground, claim it was Crusher's fault.

Remember, your parents will be watching you. Try to bring your dads along to the match, especially if they're big and burly. They can intimidate the ref and hassle the parents from St Gripewater's. Anything that helps us win is important.

Hang on, who's this old gent? You're David's Grandad, and you've been listening to my little pep talk with the lads? Football's not like in the old days when Stanley Matthews and Bobby Moore were playing? Sorry, Grandad; never heard of them ...

Nineteen
Chemistry used to be such a blast

Children enjoy my science assemblies, especially when something changes colour, fizzes, explodes, or flies around the hall. But now, with new health and safety restrictions being thrust at us virtually every week, I'm even cautious about inviting children to help with a demonstration. And when I do the experiment where the lid blows off the treacle tin to demonstrate how hot air expands, I sometimes think I should move the children to the back of the hall and give 'em all hard hats.

But it's November, and we're currently in the firework season – a time I loved as a child – and I can never resist a firework Assembly where I do a few exciting things with chemicals. Gone are the days when I could wind a piece of magnesium ribbon around a pair of scissors and ask a child to hold it at arm's length while I set fire to it, but I can always find a teacher willing to risk it.

I often wonder how I survived as a child. I loved chemistry, and long before I entered secondary school and knew what the subject was called, my little chum Clive and I were mixing explodable potions and testing them in his dad's garden shed. Heaven knows how we didn't suffocate from the fumes, let alone blow ourselves to pieces.

The thing was, you could buy an amazing range of chemicals from the local chemist. All you needed was a plausible excuse. 'My dad is showing me how to make invisible inks – have you got any copper sulphate crystals?' 'Certainly son, but when you dissolve them in water, just make sure you don't drink it. It's poisonous and it could kill you.' And that was that; the onus was on you, and if you did happen to poison yourself, there wouldn't be any mileage in your mum trying to get compensation from the chemist.

I've no idea how, but Clive always seemed to have enough dangerous knowledge to keep us living on the edge. I can remember hanging around the back of the local cinema and persuading the projectionist to give us a few offcuts of nitrate film, on the pretext that my dad had a home projector but no film to show on it. Had the projectionist known we intended to wrap it up tightly and set fire to it – it was highly inflammable and made a spectacular smoke bomb – I doubt whether he would have been so willing to give it to us.

Somehow, Clive had learned that gunpowder was made from saltpetre, sulphur and charcoal. He'd graduated to this from wrapping red-tipped matches tightly in silver foil and putting them on the gas ring, where they made a startling explosion that frightened us and caused the cat to bolt for the door (so we only did this when his mother was out shopping).

Again, the chemist readily supplied the saltpetre and sulphur, and we discovered that lighting a mixture of the two produced lethally hot bubbles. Like molten lava, they rolled down the plank of wood we were experimenting on, burning a furrow as they went. Had the bubbles dropped onto us, I suspect they would have burned their way right through our flesh in seconds.

The main problem was getting the mixture to fire up, although we soon found that Jetex fuse wire, available from toy shops and usually used to ignite model aeroplane engines, performed exceptionally well. The only downside was the cost, sixpence a tin – so a lot of empty lemonade bottles had to be taken back to the grocers to earn that kind of money.

Sadly, I lost touch with Clive shortly after he'd been grounded for emptying a can of Andrews Liver Salts into his grandmother's bedroom commode. When she'd risen in the night to relieve herself, the resulting effervescence had caused her to seek immediate and urgent medical assistance.

Health and safety might not have been there to protect us, but wow, chemistry was such fun in those days!

December

Twenty
Much ado about parking

Just when you think it'll be a straightforward day, something always happens. Take last Thursday, for example.

Premises Officer Dave cleverly packs everybody's cars into our tiny car park. Teachers tend to have small, sensible cars, so he's able to cram them in like sardines. But teaching assistants and visitors also have cars, and even teaching practice students have elderly Minis or utilitarian Vauxhalls their Dads have bought for them. Leave your car in the street opposite our school for more than ten minutes and it's likely to have gone to the crusher, so room must be found. Usually, everything's manageable.

But not last Thursday. Helen had to attend an urgent SEN meeting, and she'd allowed herself plenty of time. After five minutes, she was back in the office.

'I can't get out of the car park', she said. 'A car's blocking me.' I asked her which one.

'Oh dear,' she said, 'I'm not very good on cars. I think it's a Clio.'

Clios are popular here. We're a bit of a Clio school. Today there were four, because the visiting music teacher's got one too. Nevertheless, once we'd narrowed it down to the grey one, we were making progress. We just had to find out whose it was and get it moved. Secretary Sandra always knows who drives what, so she hurried off to ask Fiona to move her car.

'That's odd', she said. 'I can't find Fiona anywhere. I know she's here because I spoke to her at 9 o'clock.'

I suddenly remembered. Fiona was on a course until late afternoon, and she doesn't own a mobile. But hang on … whenever Fiona attends a course she leaves her keys with Dave, so we just had to ask Dave, and he'd move her car.

'It's Thursday', said Sandra. 'Dave's at the bank.'

No matter, I thought, it's the age of technology. We'll ring Dave's mobile, he'll hurry back from the bank and move the car. But no, Dave had turned his mobile off. His wife offered to run to the bank and get the keys from him. Ten minutes later she was back. On this occasion Fiona had forgotten to leave the keys with him …

There was nothing else for it; we'd have to get her back to school. We knew she'd gone to the local Learning Centre, and we had the Centre's number, didn't we? No, apparently we didn't. Well, directory enquiries could find it, couldn't they? No, unfortunately they couldn't. They had numbers for Learning Centres all over the universe, but not ours.

Then I had an idea. I'd phone our governing body clerk. She always knew things like that. A recorded message told me she'd gone to lunch. Another idea ... I'd phone some local schools. Nobody lifted the phone at the first two. A lady at the third said she was only standing in, but she knew Denise had a book listing all the offices, centres and departments in alphabetical order, and if I cared to hang on, she'd find it. By the time we'd got to 'C' we'd used another twenty minutes ... and the number she gave me turned out to be a dry cleaner's.

Meanwhile, Dave had returned and was appraising the situation. If Karen nudged her car backwards a bit, Kathy moved hers sideways a few centimetres, and Sandra inched towards the wall, Helen might just be able to get out, provided she was willing to try a few hair-raising manoeuvres.

And it worked! Another problem solved. What variety my job provides, I thought. But, within half an hour, Helen was back.

'Only two of us turned up', she said. 'They cancelled the meeting.'

Twenty-one
Not even hypnosis can help

Ah, come in Mr Smith. And what makes you feel the need for
a psychiatrist?

Well, the thing is, doctor, I'm a teacher ...

Ah, I seem to have talked to a large number of those lately.
What are your symptoms?

*Basically, I'm four months into the school year and I've forgotten
what a child is. I vaguely remember they are rather fascinating
little creatures, and once upon a time I devised wonderful
things for them to do in my classroom. Something called
exciting learning used to take place. But I don't have time for
that any more. APP, you see ...*

APP?

*Yes. Assessing Pupil Progress. It's the new system for keeping track
of my children. I do a lot of it in my PPA.*

PPA?

*Planning, Preparation and Assessment time. But that's just it.
There isn't enough of it for all the form filling I'm required to
do these days. There are 30 children in my class and I've been
up every night till four in the morning levelling their writing.
I haven't even got to Maths yet. My wife has forgotten who I
am, my neighbours think I've passed away, and I've had to sell
the cat. Haven't got time to feed it.*

Dear me, this sounds very serious. Surely the forms can't be
that demanding?

*I have an example with me. Excuse the shaky hand and the nervous
tic and the dry little cough. I'm given a set of papers like this for
every child in my class and I have to use the set to decide whether
the child has reached Level 1, 2, 3 or 4 with their writing. As
you can see, each set has 27 parameters and 130 sub-headings.
I have to consider them all. You haven't got any gin, have you?*

Sorry, no, but there's some Valium in the jar. Oh, it's all gone.
Must have had a lot of teachers in this week.

*You see, I'm bewildered by half the headings, and if I don't finish
them this week my senior managers won't be able to put all the*

data on the computer and the local education authority will be very cross.

Can't you ask your headteacher to help you?

Oh no, she never comes out of her room any more. I believe she lives in there.

But surely you know whether your children are making progress without asking a computer to cough out graphs and charts?

Of course I do, but teachers aren't to be trusted these days. That why I have to complete all these APP sheets to decide whether Charlie is low, high, secure or hopelessly insecure with each attainment focus.

Let's have a look, then. Use of connectives and subordination, sentence demarcation, time-related phrases, use of adverbials ... I see you've started shaking, Mr Smith.

Sorry, I can't help it. The very phrases cause a reaction in my underwear.

Mmm ... lexical words with more than one morpheme, orientation inconsistencies, distinguished ascenders and descenders ... Good God, whoever compiled all this rubbish? Committees who've never practised what they're preaching, presumably?

I wouldn't like to say. We're not really allowed to give a view. We're only teachers ...

But don't children write for pleasure any more? Don't they write stories and poems and little plays? Aren't they encouraged to experience the sheer joy of putting words together for a useful purpose?

There isn't the time, I'm afraid. Always the next hoop to crawl through or level to reach.

Well, Mr Smith, you're in a bad way, so here's my solution. I have a friend who's a hypnotist. He'll put you to sleep for a couple of years, by which time hopefully all this nonsense will have passed. If sanity hasn't prevailed when you wake up, I suggest you find the nearest rooftop and start shouting about it very loudly. Before it's too late for our children ...

Twenty-two
Watch out! Jobsworth's about!

Mr Jobsworth has visited. In fact, he visits several times a year, though in different guises and always at the busiest times. Usually when you're preparing for a concert, or in the middle of winter when you've got three teachers off sick.

He might be the auditor who wants me to account for every last halfpenny. Or the man who looks for asbestos when there isn't any. Or – a particularly draining two hours, this one – the health and safety lady who tells my teachers, without a trace of humour, that risk assessments for classes going to the swimming baths should include provision for sudden terrorist attack.

But today's Mr Jobsworth is a senior gent in the department of Human Resources, and he's come to see if I have the necessary 3,000 policies that will prevent us being dragged to an industrial tribunal, or sued when Mrs Smith gets stroppy because a teacher won't let her little Charlie do whatever he likes.

Mr Jobsworth makes himself comfortable, puts his checklist on his knee, and asks to see my Grievance Policy. I bring it up on the monitor, but apparently that won't do. It needs to be on paper, and filed on a shelf with the hundreds of other policies I'm supposed to have. Why? I ask. Because, he says, it's recommended procedure.

But that's just silly, I say, and what about our carbon footprint? He doesn't like being called silly, and he hurrumphs, moving to the next item on his list. Could he see my Code of Standards and Behaviour for Staff? I ask him what on earth he is talking about. Impatiently, he says he wants a document that tells him what I expect from my teachers.

Incredulous, I invite him into the corridor, telling him to look and listen. Art is everywhere. An infant class, which has just finished a physical education session, files past immaculately. The children are smiling and happy. A nearby Year 6 class is investigating friction, absorbed and interested. Down the corridor, top infants are playing maths games. Every child is on task. The corridor is a model of purposeful, enjoyable primary education. See if you can work out for yourself what I expect, I tell Mr Jobsworth.

Back in my room, I'm asked if the staff are familiar with the restraint policy. The restraint of what, I ask. Children, he says. Actually, I say, we don't do restraint. Our school's too interesting for children to need restraining. Well, he says, suppose I'm a supply teacher in one of your classrooms, and a child has gone berserk. I'd need to view your restraint policy before dealing with the child.

I say that by the time he'd read it, the child would have beaten his mates up and broken the furniture. If we had that situation, we'd use something called common sense. He harrumphs again.

I point to my computer and the 89 model policies that sit on its desktop. Do you realize, I say, that reading that lot would take at least six months? Do you also realize that a child drowned last month because two policeman wouldn't risk jumping into a lake, that their superior officer said 'procedures' had been followed correctly, and that this dreadful news merited a mere handful of words in the newspapers? Such is the state of bureaucracy we have reached.

Just then, Secretary Sandra enters. 'I'll be busy for a while', she says. 'Darren's messed himself.'

'Choices', I say to my visitor. 'Sandra has several: Darren's mum's away; Gran won't come out; Sandra can walk him home, or clean him up and risk mum suing because his trousers have been removed, or she can leave him covered in shit. What would you do?'

He didn't seem to have a policy for that.

Twenty-three
Issa just a seemple problem

Recently, a friend emailed an amusing audio clip of a customer ringing a computer repair department. He'd got his computer back and, despite the fact that he'd told the service department not to tamper with the hard disc, he discovered that all his files had been wiped. He starts very politely, but ends up screaming a bewildering array of obscenities down the phone in utter frustration.

But, last Thursday, I understood exactly how he felt.

'Something's wrong with my computer', said Secretary Sandra. I sensed an edge in her voice. All our important pupil data is held on her machine, and she'd just updated everything for the annual census. 'Don't worry,' I said, 'I'm sure we can sort it.'

Like a naughty child refusing to move, her screen sat there on her desk displaying a message that a system file was corrupted and nothing more could be loaded. So there. Ha ha. What are you going to do about that, Mister?

In fact, I wasn't too worried. I'd backed everything up onto a portable drive, and we had a recovery disc to sort the corruption out without disturbing the data files. I loaded the disc and left it churning away while I carried on making Christmas decorations. When I returned, it said everything had been successful and I could now re-boot. I did. And up came the same message as before.

Now I began to worry too. Meantime, the rich pageantry of primary school life carried on around us. Ahmed from the Reception class had been sent up with diarrhoea, Charlie had lost his coat, Ben was soaking because Aaron had sprayed him with drinking fountain water. There was only one thing for it. Stop worrying and send for the cavalry.

In our case, the cavalry takes the form of Italian Angelo, who can dissect a computer like a fishmonger filleting a kipper. He sensed the urgency in my voice and arrived within the hour.

'Ah,' he cried, 'issa seemple problim. I just replace-a the bad file.' Using diagnostics discs from his kit, he transferred some files and booted up again. The same message returned, and now Angelo looked concerned. 'Interesting', he said, in the way computer geeks do when they're completely baffled. 'Issa not such a seemple problim after all.'

He explained that he'd need to disembowel the machine, remove the hard drive and try to recover the school data in his workshop. If it was still on there, of course. Sandra blanched visibly. I wanted to cry. What if we had to type everything in again? It would take forever.

And then I remembered the portable back-up drive. We plugged it into the computer in my room and checked the data was all there. It was. But the program running it wouldn't work. Angelo tapped away, but still nothing.

'Don-a worry', he said. 'I come back sometime maybe next week. We feex eventually.'

I held his hand gently, and explained that if he couldn't feex it by tomorrow, I would be committing hara-kiri. A teacher popped her head round the door to ask something, but withdrew promptly when she saw my face.

Although my computer skills don't equal Angelo's, I took the portable drive home and sat up half the night trying to interpret messages saying that file lib.dib.exe.diddly/doo needed moving to C:/exe.lollipop.beta.bin. Eventually, around midnight, success came as things began to piece together. In the morning, elated, I plugged the portable drive into a notebook computer to re-assure Sandra we hadn't lost anything. Before my eyes, the notebook died, emitting a burning smell.

Then, just as I'd decided now was the ideal time to run screaming into the hills, Angelo re-appeared, smiling. He'd retrieved the data, and installed it on a newer computer he'd found in his workshop, which Sandra could have for a pittance if she wanted.

I'm rarely over-emotional, but, frankly, I was extremely tempted to kiss him.

Twenty-four
If it can go wrong, it will

Christmas is coming, and with it the Christmas concert. It's an event that I always look forward to. Our school has a reputation for the creative arts, and, under the guidance of my talented staff, our children always manage to delight their parents with a colourful hour of festive music, poetry and drama. So high has the standard become, our shows are like miniature West End productions.

And therein lies a problem, because we always worry about what might go wrong. Will the CD player suddenly pack up, or decide to skip a track? Will a bit of the scenery collapse? Will a child make an overly enthusiastic entrance and, like Simone did, bring half of the stage curtain with her? Will a mobile phone ring? ... and, if it does, the owner is bound to be a parent sitting in the centre of the hall where nobody can stop her having a loud conversation.

The ritual starts with an activity we call 'seating the mothers'. Some of our parents are – how to put this delicately – generously upholstered. On the other hand, our school hall is small, and since our concerts are well attended we have to use the children's chairs.

Years ago, parents would wade in amongst the chairs, scattering them as they sought a place to sit. They'd also bring snacks, umbrellas, thick overcoats – and often a baby which would cry throughout most of the show. One year, a mother brought both her current boyfriends and a six-pack of lager. We've got all that sorted now. The rules are strict and we use a large school governor to regiment the parents into neat, tight rows.

The children usually perform faultlessly, although we do have our moments, such as the year when the Angel Gabriel got his wings firmly caught in the wooden structure of the stable. As he moved position, his costume and wings remained attached to the stable, and he greeted the baby Jesus clad only in his vest and underpants. Horrified, he sought refuge behind the ox and ass.

Jason, on the other hand, wouldn't leave the stage. His teacher knew he had talent, but she had struggled to convince him he was right for the main role in the class play. Once he'd experienced the thrill of performing to his mum and auntie, who applauded and videoed his every movement, he refused to get off, repeating his song *ad nauseam* and ignoring his teacher's increasingly curt insistence that his time was up. Finally, she climbed on stage and led him firmly off, while he waved enthusiastically at his adoring relatives.

Sometimes it's the props that seem to develop a life of their own. Santa's toybox was a prime example. Beautifully constructed, it took centre-stage all ready for the Chief Elf to open, whereupon Santa's toys would come out and perform their actions for the audience. When the time came for the lid to be lifted, Alfie seemed to be struggling. 'Open the lid, Alfie', urged his teacher from the wings. Alfie fiddled frantically. 'Open the lid, Alfie!' his teacher implored again. 'I'm trying,' Alfie announced loudly and irritably, 'but the bloody lid's stuck!'

If it isn't the props, children or scenery, the hall itself can mess things up. When the roof was being repaired, we suffered the worst thunderstorm of the year right in the middle of the Christmas concert, and the rain was soon dripping into the laps of the audience. I stopped the show, shuffled the audience around, handed out waste buckets to catch the water, and told the parents that little problems like this certainly weren't going to stop the performances of their wonderful children.

There was a rousing cheer from the parents, the children carried on, and the collection of money after the show was our best ever.

January

_____
_____
_____
_____
_____
_____
_____
_____
_____
_____
_____
_____
_____
_____
_____
_____
_____
_____
_____
_____
_____
_____
_____
_____
_____
_____
_____
_____
_____
_____

Twenty-five
£355 for a day full of waffle

You take your car in for a service. When you collect it, the mechanic tells you there's a problem with the nearside rear calliper dustshield retainer. You haven't a clue what he means, but you don't want to appear a fool and you ask him to fix it. Although the retainer is really only a small metal clip, he knows you'll pay whatever he asks. He's confused you with the jargon of his trade.

It's just as bad in education. Recently, a colleague sent one of her youngest teachers on a classroom management course for a day. Afterwards, the teacher had difficulty recalling anything useful she'd learned, but she did return with a colourful, expensively produced handout. Consider this statement from it:

> In the assessment context, the use of verbal/non-verbal techniques can inform our judgements and isolate strategies we can categorize as those of assessment, as opposed to variants such as teaching or feedback.

Would that sort of thing keep Billy in his seat? Of course not. It's waffle. Rubbish. Even worse, the school paid £180, which didn't even include lunch, for the teacher to attend, and this sort of stuff was peddled all day to the dewy eyed.

Add that to the £175 for the supply teacher who covered her class for the day, and learning a little jargon became a costly experience for the school. Personally, I'd have covered the class myself and asked her to spend the time with a good classroom practitioner. She'd have learned more ... and the £355 could have been spent on extra equipment for her classroom.

Primary education seems to spend an awful lot of time re-inventing itself and designing suitable phrases to describe questionable techniques, and yet we never seem to spend enough time running with the things that really work.

If I wanted to, I could spend a great deal of money bringing consultants, advisers and 'experts' of every description into school to lecture my staff. But when I look through the lists of what's available, I'm often baffled by the lecture titles, let alone at the thought of a day struggling with the tedium behind them. What do you make of *'Building Bridges in Perspective Balancing'* or *'Targeting The Listening System'*? Precious little? Me too.

Looking back, though, perhaps things have always been like this. As an eager, dewy eyed young teacher myself in the sixties, I was concerned at how little my first class had previously achieved in Maths. I spent a lot of time teaching basic concepts, and was really getting somewhere, until the day I was visited by the local inspector, who told me, incredibly, that Maths 'wasn't about numbers'.

She said that my children – who were almost at the end of their primary years – should have been spending their maths time exploring 'real-life' issues and nothing else. Making traffic graphs with sticky paper, or constructing castles from cornflake packets to explore area, would be good places to start, she said. I wasn't sure the parents of my children would have been entirely happy, but early in your career you don't question whether an inspector has a grip on reality.

Buzz words and phrases have always been prolific in education, but never more so than now. If we're not 'Striving For Excellence', we're 'Driving Up Standards' by setting 'Smart Targets', or 'Empowering Our Learners' by offering 'Opportunities For All'. Laudable aims, usually accompanied by glossy booklets and not much else. And sometimes the phrases are merely daft. 'Outreaching Our Communities' is my current favourite. Now what on earth does that mean?

I hear there's a version of bingo currently played by young executives required to attend tedious business management courses. They decide on a group of buzz words, write them out on a grid, and as soon as the lecturer says one, they put a tick through it. The idea is to be first at crossing out a line of words, at which point you jump up and shout 'Bullshit!'

Sounds like an idea we could adopt in education, too.

Twenty-six
A film buff's admission of defeat

I have a ticketing problem.

Let me explain the context. Throughout the seventies and eighties I was an avid cine enthusiast. When I married and we moved from a small flat to a three-bed semi, I spent a pleasurable six-week summer holiday converting my loft into a mini cinema, and amassed a large collection of Super 8 films. Naturally, I incorporated my hobby into school life, and virtually from the start of my headship I've been running 'Friday Film Club' during Friday lunchtimes.

For those of us ancient enough to remember, it's rather like Saturday Morning Pictures in the fifties. Children crowd into our Viewing Room, sit comfortably on the carpet, and watch a programme of classic films on the 'big screen'. Tom and Jerry, Laurel and Hardy, Captain Marvel, Harold Lloyd, classic Walt Disney ... all are enjoyed by my excited audience of potential film buffs.

The problem lies with the ticket system. For those who want to come, the cost is 45p. Children originally paid their teachers on Mondays, collected a paper ticket on Fridays, and handed it in at the door. But paper proved impossible. Tickets were lost in the playground, fluttered away on the breeze, or were screwed into oblivion, particularly by the infants.

Laminated tickets seemed the answer, but, children being what they are, they still lost them. Or separated the plastic from the card, or put them down for a moment to find somebody had walked off with them. Or, in Simon's case, ate them. Since they were printed on brown card, his mate had convinced him they'd been made from rolled-out liquorice.

A couple of children even tried to gain entrance with homemade tickets they hoped would look genuine in the surge through the door. Unfortunately their forgery skills weren't quite up to those of Donald Pleasance in 'The Great Escape'.

The system had to change. We couldn't simply do a roll call when the children were seated; we'd lose too much film screening time. What about button badges? suggested Secretary Sandra. They wouldn't get lost or screwed up, because they'd be pinned to the children. It seemed a good idea and we ordered several packs.

The idea lasted a month. Thinking they'd be helpful, children tried to tug them off as they came into Film Club and the badges fell apart in their hands, or dropped on the floor to be trampled under a million feet. Charlie had a different take on all this. He smuggled his badge through the door and entertained himself by poking the pin into people's bottoms as soon as the lights went down.

Back to the drawing board. Objects were out. What about stamping a star on children's wrists? Simple to do, the ink wouldn't wash off and the children wouldn't need to hand anything in as they came through the door. We considered hard, drilled deep, thought outside the box, brainstormed intensely – and this plan seemed watertight. We congratulated ourselves and looked forward to Friday.

And indeed, everything was fine for two weeks. Then we noticed that the large volume of children coming into Film Club didn't tally with the smaller number who'd actually paid for tickets. Examining the stamped stars on the children's wrists, it was noticeable that some were paler than others. The children had found they could get their mates in free if they pressed their wrists together, transferring a faint but passable copy of the star.

The star-stampers were given to teachers to use for good work, and we thought again. Coloured rubber bands this time. The band could easily be slipped off the wrist and dropped in a box. Foolproof. At least, it was until last Friday, when I noticed a paper pellet zip through the projector beam and hit somebody squarely on the ear …

Self Evaluation Forms, School Improvement Plans, Targets – no problem at all. But when she visits next month, I might just ask my School Improvement Partner's advice on Film Club admissions …

Twenty-seven
A day off sick? Surely not

I wake up at six o'clock feeling terrible. It's very cold, and it's pouring with rain. I feel very much like the weather.

I'm sure I'll be fine once I get up and start moving around. I try, and I fall over. This is awful. I assume I've caught the flu and I climb back into the still-warm sheets. I'll try again in a bit, I tell my wife. She says the school can survive perfectly well without me and she brings me two aspirins and a cup of steaming tea. She fusses over me briefly – always enjoyable – and then hurries off to work.

I hate being ill. In 40 years I've only had 25 days off for sickness, and ten of those were spent recovering from a minor operation. My teachers tell me the only time my voice has a slight edge to it is when they phone in sick – which, like me, they hardly ever do. I don't expect people to be ill. And now, even though I could never make it to school, I feel guilty.

I decide to make the most of it. Since I'm always in school by 7.40 I never hear all of Radio 4's 'Today' programme. This morning I can. But a pounding headache makes me turn it off after a few minutes.

There's a thump as something lands on the bed. It's Cilla, our cat. We had no intention of having a cat, but she was young, and unwanted by her owners, and she'd sit on our patio during the summer holiday while I was refitting the kitchen. She'd eye the ham in my sandwiches and purr gratefully if I shared it with her, and things kind of went from there. I peer over the bedcover. Cilla wanders right up to my face, purrs, and pats my head with her paw. It's not sympathy; my wife forgot to let her out. I stagger downstairs and hurry back to bed, feeling dizzy from the effort.

I'm woken 15 minutes later. Bob, my neighbour, isn't at school today. He's a retired secondary teacher who still loves the job and works two days a week. He's warm, kind and humorous, and when he talks about school I imagine how enjoyable his lessons must be. His love of cowboy music doesn't endear me to him this morning, though. I tuck my head under the sheets to the strains of Frankie Laine rounding up the steers.

The dustcart rumbles down the road. Dammit, I haven't put the wheelie bin out. I hunt for dressing gown and slippers and hurry outside. I'm in time, just. It's only when I'm snuggled back under the covers that I remember I should have put the paper and card container out too, because that collection is made an hour later. Back on with the dressing gown and slippers.

The hammering starts twenty minutes later. Neighbours have had their roof replaced and the scaffolding is being removed. Poles and fixing brackets clang noisily on the ground. There's no point in trying to sleep, so I look through my school bag and find the form for the new-style school financial audits. It's 30 pages long and might as well have been written in Sanskrit for all the sense it makes.

I put it aside … and eventually drift off. I wake at two o'clock, and I feel great. It seems it can't be flu after all. Flu doesn't disappear that quickly. Then I remember I'd had a slight allergy rash at school yesterday and thrown a handful of pills into my mouth as soon as I'd got home. I check the bottle and discover it was the wrong medicine and way above a sensible dosage.

But … hooray … I'm okay and I can go to school in the morning. And I know what I'll be reading on my visit to the Nursery class. Jill Murphy's 'Peace At Last!'

Twenty-eight
Hold hands and always stay in pairs

Chatting to a friend who is a retired headteacher, we were discussing how health and safety requirements and lengthy risk assessments can discourage teachers from taking classes on trips. He described how, years ago, he'd mislaid two children on an evening visit to the Albert Hall. In those days, risk assessment was a mere twinkle in the eye of future officialdom, but there were still simple checking routines to be done, such as counting the children onto the coach – which is how he realized two were missing. In fact, they weren't far away; they'd been caught behind another party. But his heart had skipped several beats in the meantime.

Which is certainly what mine did when I lost two children on London Underground's Circle Line. I'd only been teaching for six months, and I wanted my Year 3s to visit the Tower of London. The deputy head offered to come with me, and everything had gone well, but we'd stayed too long and by the time we got to the station the rush hour had started. When we reached our stop, my deputy manoeuvred the children through the crowded carriage and onto the platform, ready to count them.

As the train moved off, I saw – with an icy horror that enveloped my entire body – the faces of sisters Hergun and Murvette pressed hard against the glass of the carriage door, as the train disappeared into the tunnel. Not only had the train taken two of my children, but they were Turkish Cypriots, recent immigrants with special needs and a mere smattering of English words between them ...

What to do? Since it was the Circle Line, we knew the train would eventually return to the same spot, but that meant waiting an hour. And what if the two children had hurried off in a panic? Should I leap onto the next train and see if they were at the next station? After a hurried discussion, we decided that the deputy should walk the children back to school, and I should alert the station master, who promised to telephone the staff at the next two stations immediately.

I hung around, biting my nails with worry. Twenty minutes later he told me that the children had been recovered two stations on.

'We's lost', they'd said to a passenger, who'd immediately taken them to the booking clerk, who'd phoned the police, who were at that very moment taking them home.

Overcome with relief, but fearful of losing my job, I phoned the deputy. She said she'd pop round and see the parents, and she was certain everything would be okay. When she arrived, Dad was sitting up in bed, clad only in vest and shorts, smiling broadly and sharing a huge portion of baked beans on a tin plate with the two girls.

I didn't sleep well that night.

Two years later, I managed a similar feat on the first evening of an Isle of Wight School Journey. It was getting dark, but the children wanted a walk on the beach and a look at the sea. When we eventually got back to the guest house, one of the children in Room 5 came and told me that Sharon didn't seem to have returned.

I suggested they look again, certain she couldn't have gone far. When she still couldn't be found, I hurried back to the beach, calling her name to the waves like a possessed Canute. Nothing. I ran back to the hotel, assuming she'd be there – but she wasn't.

I was just about to call the police when they arrived on the doorstep – with Sharon. She'd attached herself to the end of another school party, not realizing in the semi-darkness that it wasn't us. The policeman wasn't a happy bobby.

Now then, where did I put that pad of risk assessments …

Twenty-nine
The invention is fine. The service isn't

Every so often, a fascinating and useful invention arrives in the primary school classroom. The 16mm projector in the sixties. The BBC Microcomputer in the eighties. Interactive Electronic Whiteboards are the current essential classroom accessory, filled with exciting possibilities.

I've just had my final classroom kitted out with one, and I chose the supplier and installer – and even the time of year – with consummate care. Having the first few installed by the LEA-recommended suppliers the year before hadn't been a barrel of fun.

Electronic whiteboards must be linked with a projector, computer, sound system, and lots of wires that must be properly concealed, lest Charlie trips over one and Mrs Brown senses compensation in the air. And since education authorities buy equipment like this by the bucketload, lots of firms quickly join the gold rush, offering to supply all the schools in a local authority for what seems a very reasonable price indeed.

Which is fine, until the smaller firms realize they've bitten off more than they can chew. So they contract some of the work out – and the contractors may not have the same high standards as the smaller firms.

Schools then have many more people to deal with, so communications get tangled. It happened with computers, as authorities rushed to provide their schools with the latest technology. Vast amounts were spent before people had really come to grips with the equipment specifications, or realized that small children would have a tendency to poke bits of pencil into CD trays, or that the machines would be virtually obsolete within months.

Schools, in their naivety, can easily make expensive errors. Take that colour laser printer, for instance, which seemed to be the bargain of the year until it was discovered that the toner cartridges cost nearly a hundred pounds each, and both children and teachers have a habit of printing an awful lot of stuff ...

For us, things went well at first. The classrooms to receive our initial three electronic whiteboards were surveyed, and the high ceilings taken into account. The boards arrived promptly, and we waited with excitement for them to be fitted.

Then things began to go pear-shaped. The firm asked if fitting could take place in the last week of the summer term, but lots of activities were taking place and we couldn't empty three classrooms of furniture and children. I also suspected the more unsavoury elements of the outgoing Year 6 classes might fancy writing 'bum' on the whiteboards with an indelible pen. Could we, therefore, have the boards fitted at the beginning of the holiday? Yes, I was assured. That would be fine.

I drove to school on the first Monday of the holiday to make sure all was well, and found a van containing two engineers. They had a problem. The surveyors had forgotten to mention the narrow staircases in our school and they didn't think they could get their ladders up them. They might be able to haul them up the exterior of the building with ropes, but it could be dodgy, and their health and safety people weren't best pleased with the idea. They'd come back tomorrow with smaller ladders, and have another try.

Worried, I popped in on Tuesday too, and found them sitting in the car park again. The firm hadn't supplied enough trunking, and demand had outstripped supply for the power boards. They were trying to source some more, but it looked as if they might have to come from China. That would take a while. Could they come back in a fortnight's time? As far as Premises Officer Dave was concerned, they could come back whenever they liked, apart from August 15th, when he was going away for ten days. I felt an ominous grip of pessimism as I went off on holiday.

I came back again the week before school started. The screens still hadn't been fitted. Two different engineers had turned up on August 15th, to find nobody there. I phoned the firm urgently, and said we were back at school shortly, but could they phone in advance as we'd have to empty three classrooms. They appeared, unannounced, on the first day back at school – an impossible time. I sent them away again.

More phone calls, another date was decided upon, and two of our boards were finally fitted. The third couldn't be done because the projector was faulty, so they left the remaining kit and loudspeakers in the corridor. It was stolen the same evening.

It now became impossible to contact anyone by phone. Everybody was 'in a meeting'. When I did manage to order more speakers, I was told I'd have to fax the order. I tried all day, and then phoned to say I couldn't get the fax through. 'I'm not surprised,' said the voice at the other end, 'our fax is broken.' That was the point at which we decided to source our own whiteboards in future, even if it meant paying a bit more.

The final straw was the receipt of a memo reminding us that our LEA whiteboards were under a three-year guarantee. If they went wrong, all we had to do was telephone and a new one would be delivered the next day.

I assumed they'd be delivered by the flying pigs.

Thirty
An official gets me all fired up

My parents knew Bill, who worked for the railways. Bill was fastidious about time. Every day, as he parked his car in the garage at the end of his garden, he pulled a string attached to a bell in the house. This was a signal for his wife to put his supper on the table. If it wasn't there dead on time, he wouldn't eat it. God knows what he must have been like to live with.

I'm often reminded of Bill as I encounter the various officials who come to my school each year. They either park themselves in my office, expecting me to spend two hours answering their inane questions, or they wander around the school, clipboard and pencil in hand, sucking their teeth at each indiscretion before delivering a doom-laden verdict at the end of the morning. Recently, it was the turn of a fire safety officer. Fortunately I was away, helping at the Southwark Music Festival, so I didn't see the steam coming out of Premises Officer Dave's ears.

Let me put things in context. I'm the first to admit that fire safety in school is incredibly important. But my school was built in the reign of Queen Victoria, when a bucket of wet sand was cutting edge technology for the dousing of flames. The corridors are narrow and the conditions are cramped, but even the Normans would have had a job attacking the building; like many schools built in the nineteenth century, it's a stone fortress, and I'm not aware of any school like mine being burned to the ground. Indeed, the only fire I recall in one of these stone learning emporiums during the last 50 years was caused by arson – and then only because the school had foolishly decided it didn't need an on-site Premises Officer with a big dog.

Nevertheless, Mr Fire Official set about his task with tooth-grinding determination, and it was soon apparent that these gentlemen have a lexicon all of their own. Our walls were covered with 'hazardous combustibles' that needed to be removed immediately. This was a reference to the children's work that decorates all the walls and is such a feature of our school.

Next came a 'trip hazard' in the corridor, otherwise known as 'a child's coat that had fallen off its peg and dropped to the floor'.

Ah, but the coat shouldn't be on a peg in the corridor anyway. It should be in a locked cloakroom. Dave pointed out that the cloakrooms had been converted into mandatory inside toilets during the seventies, so where were we going to store the coats other than corridor coat rails?

Not my problem, said Mr F.O.

Then he examined the classrooms and halls. Hopeless, he said. Breaking every rule in the book. The school should be equipped with water sprinklers that turn on automatically as fire is detected. The kitchen should be double lined. Each hall should have automatic doors that swing shut if the temperature rises.

And those cabin hooks on the doors to keep them open as the children come in and out of Assembly? Dear oh dear. Fetch a screwdriver and get them off immediately, never mind the fact that the knob on a swinging door could take a child's teeth out. He even said the fire alarm needs completely renewing – despite its having been deemed fine just 18 months ago.

Dave pointed out that our school budget simply wouldn't stretch to £125,000 pounds worth of fire safety improvements, and using common sense didn't mean we were putting children's lives at risk.

Back came the immediate, helpful response. Not my problem.

I returned from the Music Festival just as he was leaving. Interestingly, he'd parked his car right across the fire gates.

February

Thirty-one
Snow way they didn't learn a lot

It's a very cold, but pleasant, sunny morning. Almost like early spring. Yet, just three weeks ago, a snowfall seems to have brought the country to its knees.

'Thousands of schools haven't bothered to open', shouted the media. On the radio, older people told us how, as children, they had walked 200 miles, through 15-foot snow drifts, carrying school books, sandwiches and a snow shovel – and still managed to arrive at school an hour before the whistle blew.

What wimps we are, said the commentators. No moral fibre. No get up and go. If teachers can't be bothered to get to school, what kind of example are they setting for the children? They're all going to grow up work-shy …

What they overlooked, of course, was that teachers lived much closer to their schools in those days. People didn't travel very far. And health and safety regulations were unheard of. In my second year of headship it snowed, though not enough to close the school, and the entire staff turned out at playtime to have a no-holds-barred snowball fight with the children.

Imagine that now. If little Charlie got a direct hit in the ear from Sir's snowball, his mother would be digging a pathway through the snow to the local education office. A playground ice slide? What if Maisie slips and sprains her ankle, or topples over and ruins the new coat her mother shouldn't have sent her to school in?

Well, this time my school was closed too. I live on a steep hill, and I couldn't move the car. If I'd walked through the drifts, I'd have arrived just in time to start walking home again.

All but two of my teachers were in the same position. Buses had stopped running and there were no trains. Closing was the only option. Even if a few teachers had been able to keep the school open, they could have done little except park the children in front of a television or play a few games.

But teachers, stupidly, always feel guilty if they're forced to stay at home on a school day. My wife settled down to laminate pictures for a classroom display, and I planned assemblies for the next fortnight. In the event, of course, children all over the country stayed at home, had a wonderful time playing in the snow, and probably learned twice as much as they would have done at school.

Looking out of the window, I watched a neighbour play with his children. He was still playing with them late in the afternoon. He doesn't have time to do that very often. The children next door built a massive snowman in their garden. All sorts of learning took place as they struggled to roll his head into a ball and give it the right proportions to balance on his body. And on the evening news there was much footage of families in the parks, tobogganing, skating, or just enjoying themselves in the snow.

Two days later, everything was returning to normal. There was still some snow around, and my teachers seized the opportunities: did the children know how snow was formed? That no two snowflakes were identical? That snowflakes had six points – and here's how to create a beautiful symmetrical snowflake from a piece of white paper?

Even the playground became an area of unusual interest. 'How does the snow stick so neatly on the branches?' asked Hannah. 'Look at the patterns in this slice of ice', said Oliver. And Sam, rolling a massive snowball and staggering out of the gate with it, announced that he intended keeping it in his bedroom.

I bet his mother was thrilled.

Thirty-two
Jakob and his argot of nowt

Jakob is the teenage son of my Special Needs Co-ordinator. She's a part-timer, so occasionally, when I haven't caught up with her during the day, I phone her in the evening. If she's out, the phone is usually answered by Jakob, and since I spend most of my life talking to primary-school-age children, I enjoy the opportunity for a little banter with somebody who's older. The conversation begins predictably ...

> *Ring Ring*
> 'Ullo?' This, I've noticed, is the preferred teenage method of answering the telephone.
> So I say 'Ullo'.
> And Jakob says 'Ullo, who's that?'
> 'Not telling you. Have a guess.'
> 'It's Mike, innit. D'you want me mum?'
> 'No thanks, I've been trying to get rid of her for years.'
> Jakob laughs at this. 'You're a joker, Mike', he says. 'I mean, do you want to talk to me mum?'
> 'Yes please.'
> 'She's out', Jakob says. 'She's walking the whippet.'
> 'Now Jakob,' I say, 'you shouldn't talk about your dad like that.'
> Jakob laughs that deep, growly laugh that teenage boys have, the one that makes you suspect they've been out all night on the tiles.
> 'Sorry Mike', he says. 'She'll be back in half an hour.'
> 'That's not good enough', I say. 'When the boss rings, she should be available to take the call.'
> 'Yeah, right, Mike. I'll tell her.'
> 'You realize what this means, Jakob? It means I'll have to talk to you instead.'
> Jakob gulps audibly at the other end of the phone. He considers the situation. I haven't really got time to talk to a boring old geezer, he thinks. I'm a teenager. I've got things

to do, man. I've got stuff to protest about. I've got a room to
leave in a mess. I've got music to play that's even worse than
my dad's Clash records. I need to get him off the phone as
quickly as possible, so I'll keep to words of one syllable.

'So, how are you these days Jake?' I ask.

'Yeah, I'm good.'

Teenagers never say 'I'm well, thanks.' They always say 'I'm
good.' Presumably this means that late nights, and the
filling of their bodies with junk food and various other
substances hasn't caused them to 'go bad' just yet. I change
the conversation.

'How's school?' I ask.

'Yeah, it's all right.'

'And how's the work you're doing at school? Interesting?'

'Yeah, it's all right.'

'And how's life in general?'

'Yeah, it's all right.'

'So, all in all, everything considered, things are all right, then?'

'Yeah, it's all right.' He thinks for a moment. 'How are you?'
he asks politely.

'Well, I'm good,' I say, 'apart from the irritable bowel syndrome,
and the hernia, and the creaking knee, and the difficulty in
bending to get my socks on.'

I can almost hear Jakob looking at his watch. Dear God, he's
thinking, how long can this go on?

'So, what music are you into these days?' I ask.

'Oh, well, you know, Garridge-techno, that kind of thing . . .'

'I like a bit of skiffle, myself', I say.

'Sorry, I don't know what that is.'

'It's played with washboards and a bass you make out of an
old tea chest and a broom handle. I could teach you how to
make one if you like.'

'I'm a bit busy at the moment', he says, sadly.

'I could lend you some skiffle records if you want. Have you
got equipment that plays 78s?'

'No', he says. 'I . . . er . . .'

There is a sudden, carefully controlled whoop of joy.

'Mike, me mum's home,' he says happily, 'you can talk to her now ...'

My wife has come in and caught the tail end of the conversation. 'You're a wicked bugger', she says.

Thirty-three
Is it me, or is Circle Time just loopy?

Okay, I'll admit it. I'm not a fan of 'Circle Time', though I'll probably get shot down for heresy. Although it is intended as a classroom forum for children to share views, anxieties and concerns, I don't think it offers the benefits its disciples like to claim.

Education is littered with failed fashions. Even those that have had relevance to primary education have often been misinterpreted. The 'real books' fiasco of the eighties, for example, started out as a worthwhile idea. A talented class teacher, disenchanted with the turgid text of many reading schemes, designed one of her own – using only good-quality children's books.

She spent hours grading them to ensure children would progress at their own pace, but absorb worthwhile literature at the same time. Her children made such rapid progress that the method was hailed as a reading panacea, and inspectors all over the country instructed schools to throw out their reading schemes and buy 'real books' instead, failing to appreciate that simply exposing children to decent books wouldn't actually guarantee reading success. It became known as 'reading by osmosis'. And it failed.

All sorts of successes are claimed for Circle Time in building 'the balanced child', and students coming into my school on teaching practice invariably incorporate it into their weekly routine. The children sit in a circle and perform various activities, such as saying three nice things about the person on their left, or listening to Tommy explaining why he felt it necessary to give Susan a thump at playtime, or talking about how everyone feels because somebody has written 'Your mum's a prune' on a display in the maths corner.

Now this is all well and good, but why was it necessary to invent Circle Time for it? Surely, one of the qualities of really capable class teachers is the trusting empathy they should be able to achieve with their children? Within a short time they should know them all thoroughly – and the children should feel safe, interested and comfortable in the environment provided for them.

The children should also know that their teacher will find time to help them, encourage them, laugh with them, and chat with them individually outside lesson time when there is a need for it. They are her family. They should feel a real sense of belonging and identity, and want to share her values, because an exceptional teacher is still the strongest of role models.

And call me cynical if you like, but I'm a little suspicious of the writers who know a good thing when they see one and offer books on every shade and variation of Circle Time. I found six last Saturday while rummaging through the education section of a bookshop, and I was fascinated by the warm-up activities one of them described. 'Start today's Circle Time by holding hands, and passing a "squeeze" round the circle', it said. Frankly, that would rate quite highly on my scale of pointless classroom activities.

Consultants, of course, quickly latched on to the potential goldmine. 'Solve your classroom behaviour problems', said a leaflet on my desk recently. 'Attend our course on Bubble Time, an advanced version of Circle Time.' I wondered whether you had to take along your own flannel and soap.

I've even seen a Circle Time training video in which a lunchtime supervisor was summoned to the school council circle and required to sit cross-legged on the carpet while she explained how she felt about the rudeness she was experiencing from the children. The poor lady looked extremely embarrassed and the headteacher simply looked stressed.

Perhaps if she'd had a firmer grip on the school, the children wouldn't have been rude in the first place.

Thirty-four
Society has changed. Children haven't

I don't watch very much TV, but last night I switched on to see the
News and a programme called *The Gadget Show* had just started.
Among other things, the programme was reviewing home cinema
systems, and, since I'm considering updating mine, I decided to
watch it.

Within fifteen minutes my mind was reeling. The presenters
were talking at breakneck speed and waving their arms around like
windmills in a tornado. No shot lasted longer than ten seconds,
the camerawork was frenetic, and the reviews of the home cinema
systems were so brief I learned nothing at all. I assume programmes
are compiled like this because there is an ever-present worry that the
impatient viewer might get bored and flick channels.

No wonder teachers have a difficult job. We've all noticed the
attention span of children getting shorter, and the media pander
to children just as much as to adults. And so many children watch
highly unsuitable drama, often peppered with what the continuity
announcer describes as 'strong language'. Strong? It would be more
truthful if the announcer simply said 'the following programme is
full of swearing'.

Switch on the average soap, and you'll invariably find characters
shouting abuse at each other. Watch football, and you'll be lucky to see a
match where some of the players don't shove or have a pop at each other.
Invariably, somebody will argue with the referee, and I haven't watched
a match in years in which the players aren't continually spitting on the
grass. And despite the fact that there are hundreds of television channels
to choose from, the content of many is frighteningly vacuous.

Before children join my Nursery class, the class teacher undertakes home visits to meet them and their parents, and every home
she visited this year had a huge, widescreen television. In one
lounge, there was no furniture at all, but the room contained the
biggest TV she'd ever seen. The parent didn't even bother to turn
the volume down while my teacher was trying to talk.

If it's not the TV screen children are watching, they'll be eating
dubious takeaways, playing electronic games in their bedrooms,

twiddling on their mobiles, or going onto the internet, Facebooking, Twittring and MySpacing until they fall asleep.

And it's becoming more and more difficult for parents to monitor what their offspring are watching and playing, such is the ease of accessing pornography – even on the latest mobile phones. A recent report suggested that, by the age of 13, many youngsters could have viewed around 200 strangers having sex. It really seems as if our youngsters are heading into the abyss ...

And yet ... And yet ...

When I stop to think about it, the children in my school don't really seem that much different from those of 20 years ago. Camberwell was a challenging area then and it remains a challenging area now. The changing social landscape has simply brought a different set of problems. But the children are still interesting, enthusiastic, full of humour, and fun to be with.

I stood in the hall last Thursday, listening to our orchestra, and marvelled at 40 children thoroughly enjoying playing Mozart. On Friday, I watched a Year 6 class performing a play they'd worked on this half term. It was of an exceptionally high standard, and every child in the class was involved.

I read the constant stream of letters on our website from past pupils, who tell me what they're doing now and how much they loved their time at our school. And virtually every day I see children like Jason from Reception, who staggered into my room yesterday to proudly demonstrate the submarine he'd built from a dozen cardboard boxes, complete with periscope and turbo-driven propellers.

Perhaps, after all, we shouldn't worry too much just yet.

Thirty-five
We do it all for you, children

Dear Children,

Thank you for letting us come to your school last week for your Ofsted inspection. (Well, if we're honest, it wasn't up to you, was it? We just rang Mrs Smith, your headteacher, and said we were coming, but saying 'thank you' is what's called 'professional etiquette'. That's French for 'good practice', a phrase we use a lot in education these days.)

As you know, as well as giving our inspection report to Mrs Smith, we also have to write a letter to you, telling you what we thought of your teachers. That's called 'treating you as the stakeholder'.

I expect you've been wondering why your teachers looked so grey during the inspection. Well, this is because none of them had slept since our phone call, and they'd been in school every night and all weekend making sure every second of every lesson we might be likely to see was accounted for.

The thing is, you see, if your teachers aren't up to the job we put the school in a thing called 'special measures', and then we come and visit them over and over and over again until they're making a better job of things. Or until the headteacher pulls his own leg off and gets led away by some people in white coats.

After all, you have an entitlement, you see. We inspectors want you to have the very best education the Government can afford, with any money that's left over after it has paid us and lots of other important people called 'consultants' and 'advisers' and 'experts'.

That's not to say we get everything right, of course. Miss Trembling shouldn't have been visited 28 times on the first day of the inspection, and she bore that with great fortitude.

Unfortunately, because she was shaking like a wobbly jelly by the end of the afternoon, we could only give her a 'moving towards satisfactory but unfortunately somewhat inadequate' grading, even though Mrs Smith says she's normally a super teacher who works very hard and is loved by her children and their parents. Hopefully, we shouldn't have done her any lasting damage, and she'll soon come off the Valium.

Some of you thought I yawned a lot during the lessons I saw. I assure you I wasn't bored. I have a medical affliction that causes me to take in occasional gulps of air. However, I do apologize for one of my inspectors falling asleep and dropping his clipboard, because the hamster Janet had taken out of its cage was obviously very frightened and you got very grubby chasing him all over the floor on your hands and knees. That distracted you from your lesson, and we could only grade Mrs Gibbons as 'mainly inadequate with the occasional satisfactory tendency towards average'. I'm sure Mrs Smith will buy Janet a new hamster, and she'll stop crying soon.

We were very impressed with Mrs Burridge when smoke came out of the monitor in the ICT suite. ICT can be such a funny thing, can't it? We thought Mrs Burridge got you out of the room very quickly once she'd forced Tommy out of the big cardboard box. She wasn't able to complete her lesson, so we could only grade it as 'bordering on the inadequate with an incomplete plenary', but we think Tommy was clever to find his own shelter. I'm sure he is gifted and talented.

Now, we were a little worried that many of you were unfamiliar with your personal targets. Indeed, some of the three-year-olds in the nursery didn't even understand what they were. We've told your teachers to explain about targeting and tracking, and assessing for income and outcome with differentiation, which I know you'll find just as interesting as we do.

Finally, please don't worry, your teachers will eventually lose that haunted look and stop walking into walls. We shan't be back for three years, because we've got lots of other headteachers to go and see. If we can find any.

Yours sincerely, Rosa Klebb

Reporting Inspector

Thirty-six
Careful now … you'll get sold down the river

I bet there's one thing prospective headteachers aren't taught at the National College of School Leadership. How to deal with persistent salespeople.

Okay, everybody has to earn a crust, but manufacturers of all kinds of equipment know that schools are a ready market with guaranteed funding. They're also reliable institutions moneywise, so if you sell a school something, you're unlikely not to be paid. Hence the reason schools will receive at least one call from a photocopier salesman every week, another from somebody offering to update and service the computers because if you bought them last month they're probably obsolete, and yet another call from a new supply teacher agency, because supply agencies do very well indeed at the moment and have become a growth industry. That's aside from the companies trying to sell you software, insurance, toilet fresheners, playground equipment, fire safety checks, kits to cope with Ofsted and a million other things you don't really need.

At my school, most calls of this kind go through Secretary Sandra's office, and she's a dab hand at dealing with them. Refuse to give your name and the nature of your business, and you'll never be passed through to me. You'll be told I've only just gone out, or only just come in, or just about to go out again. Or that I've got a bad leg. Or I'm dealing with a difficult parent, and she tends to talk a lot, so please phone back next year. The persistent ones do keep ringing back, and if they happen to catch me, I tell them I've just gone out.

Come to think of it, perhaps a course on safeguarding headteachers against high-pressure salespeople is exactly what the NCSL should be including in their courses, because avoiding the pitfalls is a hell of a steep learning curve and I've certainly made a few blunders in my time.

Like the day, early in my headship, when a gentleman called at my office and said he could cut my fuel bill by 20 per cent. Funding was difficult in those days, and fuel bills a worry. All he needed to do, he said, was fit his firm's special device to the boiler. My Premises

Officer was interested, and we paid up. The salesman returned a month later, jiggled with a little meter, and said yes, everything was fine and we'd soon see a reduction in our bills. We did. It was about 2 per cent. Far worse than that was a local authority memo saying that schools should be wary of salesmen with fuel saving devices, because they could wreck the boiler ...

Computers were another stumbling block. When we planned our original computer suite, I wondered how we were going to afford it, until a small computer installation company phoned and said that since they only dealt with schools they were cheaper. We duly paid what seemed a very reasonable sum for an impressive looking installation, but within six months the computers began to fail and one of the monitors exploded. Worse, the company had gone bankrupt, and every engineer we called in pursed his lips, sighed, and said 'Who sold you this lot?'

These days, I'm a wise old bird and nobody's likely to sell me down the river without a paddle. Nevertheless, with the slickness of e-advertising, the pressure is really on, and when I fire up my computer in the mornings there'll be at least thirty emails trying to flog me something. If I had to award a prize of the month for seizing the moment, it would have to go to the company which, at the height of the swine flu scare, was selling portable pupil isolation suites. Only six grand, and guaranteed to keep affected pupils safe until their parents could collect them.

I wonder if they do an isolation suite for besieged headteachers ...

March

Thirty-seven
Suffering from stress? Hang upside down!

Last Friday, high above the 300 children assembled in our school hall, three of my teachers hung upside down from the gymnastics ropes and ladders, reciting poetry. Why do I mention this? Because I want to talk about stress. What has hanging upside down while entertaining children got to do with stress? Bear with me ...

A short while ago a journalist rang me and asked if she could talk to me about teachers and stress. What percentage of teachers did I think suffered from it? What caused it, and what could be done about it? And did I know that the government was thinking of requiring schools to complete a staff stress audit?

For a moment I thought it was a touch of March madness, or maybe an early April fool. But no, as well as being required to undertake audits of our finances, targets, standards, gifted and talented, health and safety procedures – to name but a few – it seems we might have to add stress to our lists.

Now, I don't want to make light of the issue. Surveys show that teachers are under stress as never before, and I'm pleased that the government is showing some concern. But why are they under so much stress? Because the government makes so many demands on them in the first place, many of them related to the constantly higher targets that schools are asked to achieve, and the battering from dubious inspection procedures.

Sadly, many headteachers these days have become mere executives. Few do any teaching or spend enough time with the children. There are constant forms to be filled in, standards to drive up, meetings to attend.

Most primary schools (not mine) also have deputy headteachers who do not teach, and some have 'assistant headteachers' as well. These senior people don't come into contact with children very often either – indeed, some actively avoid them – because they spend most of their time either observing and assessing other teachers, or rigorously checking and marking lesson plans before the lessons are delivered. Then they check the summaries of the lessons afterwards.

I haven't a clue why all this is necessary. I am constantly aston-ished at the depth of planning some teachers are asked to do, and the manner in which they are not allowed to stray, even minutely, from these plans. Presumably, today's educational consultants would tell you that rigorous planning down to the finest detail is essential for a successful lesson, but children are human beings with interesting views, and this kind of rigidity gives no opportunity for the lesson to include some alternative and informative directions as it goes along.

Personally, I think the harder you lean on teachers, and the more prescriptive you make their work, the more resentful, ineffective and stressed they become. I appoint teaching staff with great care, and then I place enormous trust in them; I don't look at their planning, I don't monitor them, I don't put them under constant observation, and I don't place demands on how long they stay after school. I then find I'm richly rewarded. They're never absent from school, they work exceptionally hard, and the children love school because our curriculum still retains a huge element of fun.

Which is why the three teachers were hanging upside down on the last day of our annual Poetry Week. They thought it would amuse the children, while having a thoroughly good time themselves. Good job the health and safety officer wasn't doing an audit that day ... although he'd have been the only adult in the building suffering from stress.

Thirty-eight
Put to the test getting the tests

I probably spend half my time in school grappling with bureaucracy.

This morning, all I'm trying to do is order this year's Key Stage 1 tests. I find the Qualifications and Curriculum Agency website and tap in my email address and password. Simple. Should have everything sorted before Assembly.

I get a message saying that something I've typed isn't correct, so I try again and get the same message. I know the email address is correct, so I phone to check the password.

A pleasant lady answers, and asks for the school's Department of Education number. Then she asks me to confirm the school's name and address, just for security purposes. That all seems okay, so she asks my name and my job title. Yep, that's all fine too, and she wants to know how she can help. I explain the problem, and she tells me I can't use last year's password. They need changing every year, and I must compile a new one.

Back on the website, I think of a new password, one I'll remember easily, and I confirm it in the next checkbox. One click, and I can complete this test ordering and get off to Assembly. It doesn't work, so I phone again. A different lady answers, asks for the school's DoE number, and could I please confirm the school's address and who I am. Just for security purposes.

Then she tells me I can't choose any old password. If I care to look at the site carefully, it tells me the password must contain at least eight characters, with upper and lower case letters, numbers and symbol characters. I also have to copy a hard to read security coding that appears on the screen.

Time is at a premium, so I return two hours later and construct a password on paper before typing it in. Then I copy the additional security code and press submit. A message in red tells me it hasn't worked. More than a little irritated now, I phone again. Sorry sir, but we can't answer any questions until you have given the school's DoE number, a confirmation of the address and your job title. For security purposes, sir.

The lady sympathizes with my frustration, and says their controllers will reset the screen and email me a new, foolproof password within 24 hours. She is as good as her word, and I type the new one in. It doesn't work.

This is the stuff of stress, so I go away, have some coffee, do lots of other jobs, and return to it the next afternoon. I telephone and say, look, all I want to do is order some tests. Can't I please, oh please, just do it over the phone? Sorry sir, I'm told. We aren't permitted to do that. However, when there are continuing problems with passwords, we do accept telephone phone orders, although it's us that'll have to ring you, and we can't do that until later next week. For security purposes, you understand. Could I, then, speak to your supervisor? Sorry, sir, she's gone home. It's after five.

I put the phone down and stare at the computer screen in sheer disbelief. Who, I wonder, is the raving idiot responsible for this ludicrous level of so-called security? It's bad enough that our infants are subjected to these awful tests, but breaking into Fort Knox would be a doddle compared with getting hold of a set of them. And why this ridiculous insistence on such complex passwords? I can only assume the boxes of tests are so highly prized that the underworld would give an arm and a leg to get hold of them.

I give up and go to Sainsburys. At least the PIN number on my credit card only has four numbers. Even I can handle that.

Thirty-nine
Don't treat pupils as consumers

Last week I heard something that worried me.

I was chatting to a teacher whose son is currently at secondary school. He'd been taught by a newly qualified teacher that day, and the class had been required to evaluate the teacher's geography lesson. This was done verbally, the children pointing out the good and bad parts of the lesson, and then via individual 'evaluation forms'. At the bottom was a space for giving the lesson a mark out of ten.

This seems very odd to me, and just a trifle sinister. Naturally, the children in the evaluation group had widely differing views. One child thought the lesson 'brilliant'. Another said there wasn't enough 'entertainment and stuff'. One thought it was 'really boring', but qualified that by saying he hated geography anyway.

Useful, or even appropriate, feedback? I wouldn't have thought so. I love MG cars and I've driven them for years. Some motoring correspondents hate them. But who's to say their views are more valid than mine? Hi-fi is another of my passions, and I recently read a rave review of a new amplifier in an audio magazine. A different magazine, reading between the lines, thought it was awful. Both reviews were written by respected audio journalists, so who was right? A prospective purchaser would surely have been bewildered. So what should he do? Go and listen to one and then make up his own mind, I'd have thought.

And that's what I think the young teacher should have done. After all, he's had training and undertaken several teaching practices. Surely he should know whether the lesson he's prepared is likely to be any good? And if he wasn't sure, why not seek the advice of another teacher whose lessons and teaching style he admired?

But I suspect I know the answers to these questions. These days, we're supposed to think of the child as 'the consumer' or 'the stakeholder'. What truly awful descriptions these are. No longer is a child a small person with a unique, relatively unformed and fascinating view of the world around him. Now he's supposed to be an adult in miniature, with the corresponding reasoning power, knowledge and experience of an adult.

I accept that we want to get as far away as possible from the days when children were seen and not heard, but let's retain a little common sense. Children look to adults – particularly to their parents and teachers – to offer a secure, loving environment tempered by wisdom and experience. A parent who uses the child as an equal, friend or confidante usually ends up with a highly insecure youngster.

For the same reason, I have a problem with the current notion of 'Pupil Voice'. Many local education authorities issue an annual questionnaire for children. The idea is that the LEA collates the information and then issues a folder of graphs purporting to show, for example, whether bullying is a major problem across its schools.

It seems a shaky premise to me. However simple and straight-forward the compiler tries to make the questions, many children still struggle to interpret them. Even 'Are you bullied in school?' can easily be misunderstood; a minor falling out with friends can cause a child to say she's being bullied. And 'Are you happy in school?' seems particularly daft. A child's world is of the moment; full of joy one day and angst the next.

A caring, well run school will always be listening to children sensitively. And if an LEA needs to thrust regular questionnaires at schools I'd say its officers need to visit them more often.

They'd soon find out what's working. And what isn't.

Forty
No harm in some rough and tumble

I stopped a playground fight yesterday. Obviously copying the professionals, two boys had been arguing over who had scored a goal, and a mild bout of shoving had quickly developed into something a bit more serious.

For all the health and safety rules in place these days just in case Mrs Smith sues, many boys undeniably enjoy the occasional tussle. But then, as a youngster, so did I. When I was fourteen, I got into a wresting match with a boy called Anthony and – I've no idea how – threw him spectacularly over my shoulder. It astonished Anthony, and it certainly impressed my classmates, who immediately and inexplicably dubbed me the best wrestler in the school. Fortunately, I was never asked to repeat the performance.

But then, I'd grown up in the Boy Scouts, and how we didn't emerge from Monday evening meetings in a swathe of bandages I'll never know. We did all the important things such as learning how to pitch a tent, catch a rabbit and tie a bowline-on-the-bight, but the highlight of the evening was games hour, when we were divided into teams and all civility was dropped.

A classic game was a little divertissement known as 'Fight For The Chalk'. Two rectangles were drawn on the floor, one at each end of the room, and a circle was drawn in the centre. A lump of chalk was placed in the circle. The boys were divided into two teams and they sat facing each other, stretched out between the rectangles. The boys in the teams were given corresponding numbers, and you sat cross-legged on the floor waiting for your turn to play.

If your number was called, you leapt to your feet, grabbed the chalk, and ran to make a mark inside your team's designated rectangle, thereby scoring a point. The only problem was your opposite number. He'd be trying to do the same, so you had to fight extremely hard for chalk possession. This meant grappling energetically with your opponent until you'd got his head firmly jammed between your legs. Then you squeezed, while trying to prise his fingers open – a process that could take a good ten minutes, with much egging on being done by your mates.

If you weren't too keen on the fight element of the game, the tactic was to sit still for a fraction of a second too long, let your opponent score, and then pretend you hadn't heard your number called. It was an accepted way of saving face.

Even worse was a ferocious two-team game known as 'Bung The Barrel'. One team lined up at the end of the hall and each boy bent down, placed his head under the crutch of the boy in front, and held his legs tightly. The other team, one by one, took a running jump onto the backs of the crouching boys and then energetically bounced up and down, trying to make the crouched row collapse. If, by some miracle, you withstood the bouncing and didn't fall, you became the team to jump in the next round. It was the lesser of two very grim evils.

We all thought it was tremendous fun, and I don't remember anybody being carted off to hospital. But how times change. Recently, I read about a group of Scouts who erected an aerial runway on a camping trip. The Scout leader had fully equipped the boys with hard hats and harnesses when two louts gatecrashed their enjoyment and climbed on the runway. One fell off and injured himself, whereupon his mother successfully sued. Unbelievably, the Scout leader was told he should have forced the louts to wear protection.

Obviously, the judge had never played 'Bung The Barrel'.

Forty-one
Why we all needed a shower

Four years ago, around this time of year, Amid, aged seven, came to us from a school in a neighbouring LEA. Continually in trouble, his work had suffered, and he'd become rude at home. His mother had tried our school originally, but lived too far away. Then a child in his age group had left, and I was able to offer a place.

We found him difficult too, but a year with an exceptional teacher changed him completely. 'My mum likes this school', he said proudly one morning. 'She says my brother's going to start in September.'

And that would have been fine. Except that Rahmid had extreme special needs. Born prematurely, with a section of his gut missing, he wasn't expected to survive, but surgeons effected a partial solution by connecting his stomach to a colostomy tube and feeding him using a special machine. The first three years of his life were precarious, but he progressed, and was able to attend a nursery for a year. At which point mum decided he should come to us.

The SENCo and I visited his nursery. He was constantly supervised by adults and, perhaps unsurprisingly, extremely indulged. His language when he couldn't do as he wanted could best be described as ripe.

We had a dilemma. We felt unable to admit a child with such extreme needs. Compared with the space at his nursery, our Reception classrooms were tiny. His statement of special needs didn't offer many support hours, and we'd have to have an extremely capable classroom support assistant. Although we'd been told Rahmid was only incontinent occasionally, we weren't convinced. And we were unhappy about the feeding machine, which the class teacher and support assistant would have to work. What if it went wrong?

We decided to make a stand. I refused to take him without adequate support, annoying the nursery he was attending because the staff were unwilling to keep him there. In a bid to hurry matters forward, the LEA offered additional money, but not full time support. Once again I refused.

I was then visited by people from the LEA, who weren't very happy. Inclusion of children with extreme special needs is a popular government theme these days, and I was refusing to include. I pointed out that inclusion was fine by me, but not without money and appropriate specialist support. I wasn't prepared to do it on the cheap, and that was that.

But I did have a suggestion. We had a disused shower room, and if the LEA funded its refurbishment to deal with the incontinence, and paid for full time support, I'd guarantee Rahmid the schooling he needed and deserved. Since Mum refused to consider any other school, and I wasn't budging, the LEA agreed, and Rahmid joined us in the summer term to acclimatize.

We had a hell of a time. The incontinence was far worse than expected, we couldn't find a suitable support worker, and the feeding machine often broke down. Furthermore, now that he was with us, the support agencies seemed to have lost interest and we were on our own. Nevertheless, the skill and dedication of his young class teacher and the SENCo worked wonders, and we began to see huge changes in Rahmid.

Once the shower room was ready, things took a leap forward, especially as he was eventually able to come off the feeding machine during the day. Now we're three years on, and anyone visiting his classroom would find a happy little boy, warm, caring and enthusiastic about learning. His mother tells me he often wakes her early in the morning and whispers 'Is it time for school yet?'

Sometimes, it really pays to dig your heels in.

Forty-two
The skip that wouldn't leave

Funny how a headteacher's day can be filled with anything but education.

We've achieved Healthy School status and, because cycling to school is something we encourage, we'd applied for a grant to buy a modern, lockable unit holding up to 20 bicycles. The application was successful and the unit was delivered and installed with remarkable efficiency in just two days. I've rarely known building work go so smoothly.

The only problem was the skip, full of bits of metal, excavated playground asphalt, piping and plastic left over from the installation. Not to worry, though, said the workmen, it would be collected well before school on Thursday morning.

I should have known things are never that simple ...

The skip was still in the playground when I arrived on Thursday, so at 9.30 Secretary Sandra put through a hasty call to the installation company. Could they collect the skip immediately, because with children around there were health and safety implications. Ah, they said, we're not actually responsible for the skip. We just carry out the installation. That's down to the people at the local education authority and the main contractor. They would have ordered the skip from a different firm.

Premises Officer Dave noted the phone number on the side of the skip. 'I'll phone and get it picked up before lunchtime', he said. 'Meantime, I'll put chairs round the skip to stop the children going near it.'

Chairs, however, weren't enough to deter Jason and Andrew. These two could unscrew the inscrutable. Put into Colditz, they'd have tunnelled out within the hour. And a skip full of interesting bits and pieces was simply too much to resist.

Five minutes into playtime, and Andrew was fashioning a robot from the sharp-edged scraps he'd retrieved. Ten minutes into playtime and I'd received a message that Josie was lying in a corner of the playground with a huge bump on her forehead, caused by Jason throwing a lump of asphalt he'd taken from the skip. It had to be Josie, I thought. Her parents, sitting at home all day with little to do, are the sort who complain at the slightest provocation. It gives their day a focus.

Fortunately, when I got to the playground, Josie was running around unharmed. It was true Jason had been chasing her, she said, but she'd been pretending about the lump on her head bit. I explained that it wasn't really a good thing to pretend about. When I found Jason, he assured me, as Jason does, that he'd intended to conduct a scientific experiment and needed a piece of asphalt. And no, sorry, he hadn't realized that the chairs around the skip were to stop people going near it.

At 11.00, Dave came to my room, frowning. He'd phoned the firm and there was a simple reason why the skip hadn't been collected. Nobody had paid for it. What's more, if it wasn't paid for by three o'clock they'd come to school and retrieve the skip, but empty its contents onto the playground. If we wanted the rubbish removed, the school would have to pay for the skip hire.

More anxious phone calls. The skip firm blamed the installers, the installers blamed the contractors, and the contractors blamed the LEA – until the skip firm checked their records again and found the payment had been made after all. They promised a lorry before lunchtime, which was fine, except that I had to rush around getting everybody to move their cars so that the lorry could negotiate the narrow entrance to the car park.

The only people sorry to see the skip go were Jason and Andrew. If it had still been there at hometime, I'm sure they would have happily emptied it and taken the contents away with them …

April

Forty-three
Always game for a laugh

One of the joys of working with young children is that they are great fun to be with. An appreciation of their very individual humour is an essential item in a good teacher's toolkit, and a day rarely goes by without my teachers sharing an amusing comment made by a child. Take Thomas, for example, who returned from illness on the initial day of our last Ofsted inspection, unaware of the visitors. "Ere', he said, spying an inspector hovering outside the classroom door. 'Oo's the bald geezer standin' in the corridor?'

Children also thoroughly appreciate humour in their teachers, and when I'm appointing a new member of staff, humour is just as essential as the list of qualifications. And with a tongue firmly planted in the cheek, there's a great deal of fun to be had in a primary school, especially if you're at school on April Fool's Day.

Like the time I convinced the Juniors, in Assembly, that I spent my holidays deep sea diving. Digging the garden that weekend, I'd found a piece of wood with some decorative carving, and I told the children it was part of a handrail from Columbus's fourth ship, the Avril Imbecilio.

I explained how I'd wrestled the artefact from the mouth of a Great White while deep sea diving during half term off the coast of Spain. It had then been identified by my 106-year-old grand-mother, an expert in seafaring matters. The younger children's mouths dropped open, and even Year 6 looked as if they wanted to believe the tale, but they'd heard this sort of thing from me before. After the Assembly Andrew examined the piece of wood disbeliev-ingly, and then correctly identified it as a bit of grubby picture rail, just like the one in his living room.

On another occasion, I told the children the local education authority had been so delighted with their work they'd sent a burger van to the school. At this very moment in time, I announced, it was being driven into the playground ready to dispense free chips, beefburgers and a new frothy green drink named after the lady who'd invented it, April Thirst.

I asked one of the teachers to look out of the window. Quickly realizing what I was doing, she said the van was indeed just drawing into the car park. After leaving Assembly somewhat quicker than usual, the children were halfway down the stairs, straining to see the van out of the window, when many realized what I'd done and hurried back to remonstrate! They forgave me when they realized I'd bought a huge bag of toffees as compensation for fooling them ...

Recently, another opportunity arose which I simply couldn't resist. A Year 5 class was busily displaying its skills with our new vaulting horse, and I asked them whether they knew about the trophies I'd won for my mid-air triple somersault vaulting. They were astonished – and exceptionally eager when I offered to demonstrate. I stood in front of the horse ready for the run-up across the hall, having arranged to be interrupted by Secretary Sandra pretending there was an urgent phone call for me.

The following week, just as I was about to perform my run-up, I'd arranged for Premises Officer Dave to say I needed to inspect a broken door downstairs. Then, during their next lesson, I read out a doctor's letter, saying that unfortunately I wouldn't be fit to perform for three weeks, as I'd twisted my leg abseiling down the side of St Paul's Cathedral.

Trouble is, the children are suspicious now, and the three weeks are almost up. It looks as if I might have to put my shorts and trainers on after all ...

Forty-four
An idiot's guide to secure testing

Had to have the armed guard out last week. The school was closed on Wednesday, and the building carefully cordoned off. The Premises Officer was put on full alert, and teachers were informed that this was a high security operation needing the utmost sensitivity. What was the cause of all this commotion?

This year's Key stage 2 test papers were being delivered.

Okay, I'm joking. But it seems the Department for Education and its contractors constantly feel they need to spell everything out to me in excruciating detail on the assumption, presumably, that I am a twit. Yes, of course we don't want boxes of test papers just dumped in the ground floor corridor by the postman, where all and sundry could take a pair of scissors to the boxes and voraciously run their eyes over the tests. We'd have the corridors full of people who'd died from boredom, for heaven's sake.

But I could hardly believe the long list of instructions that came with the tests, telling headteachers exactly what methods should be used to make sure the packets aren't opened before they're supposed to be.

First, somebody has to sign for the parcels. Not any old Tom, Dick or Harry, mind. It needs to be the headteacher, or a senior member of staff. And not just any senior member: the person has to be especially appointed to that task. Miss Robinson, you are appointed as test receiver for 2011. I trust you have the ability to sign your name legibly? Oh, thank you, headmaster, this a role I've wanted for many years ...

The boxes then have to be opened and the packets checked – making sure it's done by committee just in case somebody nicks one – after which it is permissible to inform the headteacher that everything seems to be in order. Should something be missing, it must be reported to the tests distribution helpline without further ado. Bearing in mind last year's little difficulties, that's if you can get hold of anybody, of course.

The next stage is to store all the boxes of tests in a location that is kept locked. Definitely not, we're told, in a room where there is ICT equipment, because such rooms tend to be targeted by burglars. 'Ere, 'Arry, we've fallen on our feet, lad. Leave that Topstar five million gigawatt multi-drive computer where it is. There's a box of SATs papers over 'ere. That'll fetch a fortune down the Frog and Nightgown ...

Now the actual lock has to be considered. The padlock and chain you put round your bicycle won't do at all. It needs to be a high-quality lock, of five levers. I summoned my Premises Officer immediately, who discovered that our secure location only has a lock with three-and-a-half levers, so I dispatched him in haste to Homebase to buy an updated one, before Year 6 had a chance to get their jemmies ready.

A list of the bleedin' obvious follows: don't let people wander into the storeroom; keep the key in a safe place; keep a check on who goes into the room; compile a register to sign keys in and out. I'm even supposed to conduct two daily spot checks, just to make sure everything is okay. Sandra, synchronize watches, step out into the corridor and keep an eye out for lurkers, please; it's 11.17 and time for my morning spot check.

Finally, I'm told that the distributing contractor has fully briefed the national crime prevention officers' network about the security of test materials. That's a relief, then.

I'm worn out after reading all this. And the tests haven't even started yet ...

Forty-five
A committee to crack a nut

I wasn't a particularly well-behaved child. Usually, my mother talked to me about what I'd done, and I only remember her smacking me on two occasions. Both, such as the time I caused an elderly neighbour to jump out of her skin when I lit a firework behind her, were well deserved. I think I grew up to be a reasonably well-adjusted adult.

But these days, it's difficult to comprehend the lunatic lengths we go to when a child does something wrong. The stark reality was brought home to me yesterday by a letter a secondary school colleague showed me. It was going to be sent to Kim's parents. Kim, it seemed, was a very naughty twelve-year-old, about to be permanently excluded.

The school had gone to extraordinary lengths to avoid this, but had finally run out of ideas. When she first started to misbehave, Kim had been placed on daily report, initially to her form tutor and then to the head of year. Later, several pastoral plans had been individually developed for her. They hadn't worked. Then, mentoring and counselling from an external clinical psychologist. That hadn't worked either, so a consultant had organized a special routine to help her when she encountered difficulties during lessons. The consultant presumably walked away with his cheque without giving any guarantees, because Kim's behaviour simply worsened.

She spent some time in a special referral unit, and then the school tried to re-integrate her with the help of an independent behaviour advisor. Kim and her parents signed a special 'behaviour agreement'. No change, so the school devised a unique support plan, with an LEA representative being called in to agree it.

None of these strategies were successful, and Kim continued to be insolent, defiant and aggressive. In desperation one morning, a teacher asked Kim if she could simply go to her class and stop shouting. Kim became even louder, called to her mates to watch her, and took a large carton of orange juice from her bag. She hurled it with extreme force at the opposite wall, causing the contents to shower over everybody. She then threatened to beat up anybody who came near her.

Despite this appalling behaviour, 'procedure' had to be followed. There had to be a meeting with the governing body, and a checklist of 20 criteria must be discussed before any action could be taken. Had there been appropriate early intervention? Was the child responding to provocation, bullying, racial or sexual harassment? Had achievements (dear God!) been rewarded? And on it went. If any of these criteria hadn't been followed, Kim's parents could have had a field day.

And then, of course, there are the child's rights. If, for example, the parents thought that the exclusion related to a disability Kim had, then they could consider whether 'disability discrimination' had taken place, and take appropriate action against the school.

As far as I can see, the whole system has gone barking bloody mad. Can you imagine what all this has cost? Not just in money, but in teacher hours, form filling, letter writing and stress for everybody concerned. It's a wonder there's any time left for the children who do want to learn.

And is it possible – just possible – that a good smack at an appropriate point would have been a darn sight more productive? My mother would have thought so.

Forty-six
Don't trip over the rules and regulations!

Our Year 5 children have just returned from a School Journey to the Isle of Wight.

When I was a sprightly young teacher, I used to run Isle of Wight School Journeys too. But in those days, we didn't have to worry about risk assessments, crates of medicines, and an adult to every one-and-a-half children. It all seemed so much easier.

When my imagination runs riot and I consider all the things that could go wrong, I'm surprised my teachers even agree to go on a School Journey. But they do, everybody has a thoroughly enjoyable time, and accidents and incidents are always minimal.

Which is a relief, because I've just received my local authority's new Policy and Procedures for Off Site Visits, Edition One. Having read it, I think I'd be hesitant about taking children to the end of the road, let alone such a hazard-laden place as the local park, or, heaven forbid, on an Underground train where they could get chewed up in the escalator, fall off the platform, or have their hearing severely impaired by the noise of a train emerging from the tunnel.

The document starts by saying how much the authority values the LOtC agenda. Yep, I hadn't a clue, either. It's the acronym for 'Learning Outside the Classroom'. The LEA has even set up an on-line notification system called EVOLVE to ensure that visits are planned in a methodical way for a 'safe experience'. It wouldn't be sensible, you see, to charge parents for an Isle of Wight trip unless you'd actually organized somewhere on the Isle of Wight for the party to stay. And it would be sensible if the place wasn't on the edge of a cliff, because that could be hazardous.

The document has 42 packed pages. Page 4 offers a helpful acronym guide, so if you aren't quite sure what an ESRA is, all is explained. It's an Event Specific Risk Assessment. And just in case you thought ALF was the name of the bloke leading the expedition, it isn't. It's an Activity Leader Form.

Then we're given a list of important rules for the EVC (Educational Visits Coordinator) because, like the Gifted and Talented Coordinator, every school is supposed to appoint one.

The rules offer many surprises: the person must be competent to organize and lead a visit. That comes as quite a revelation, doesn't it? As well as the other 21 things they have to be good at, they'll also be required to keep lots of records, so they'd better be good at form-filling. But then, since teachers spend so much time filling in forms anyway, I suppose that's a given.

No document of this type is complete without a flow chart, and this is no exception. You start at the box that says 'Are you planning an Off Site Visit'. Yes, you say, I am. That's why I'm reading this form. So you go to Box 2, asking if an external provider will be used. And so on through a dozen boxes of the bleedin' obvious. Answer them correctly, and you're told 'The Visit May Proceed'. By now, I bet you're thinking I'm making this up.

And that's before you get to the risk assessment itself. Incredibly, there are multiple types of risk assessment, all with silly names. You've got generic, event specific and on-going dynamic. Naturally, there's much additional guidance for all this on the Department for Education's website, but it would take you so long to read you'd never actually get to the Isle of Wight.

I'd love to climb into the minds of the people who write this stuff and see what makes them tick. On the other hand, perhaps not. I'd need a comprehensive risk assessment before going there.

Forty-seven
Hunch that unearthed a star

I'm very cautious when I appoint new teachers. Usually, they'll have undertaken an eight-week final teaching practice at our school, and they'll be a known quantity well before the interview. But, just occasionally, chance plays a hand.

I first met Alex when I went to Goldsmiths College in London to give a talk to students who were about to begin their teaching careers. I'd taken one of my own teachers who'd just completed her NQT year, which she'd thoroughly enjoyed. Alex had been invited too, and my teacher knew him well. They'd trained together, and she introduced me.

It was obvious that Alex had experienced an appalling first year. He'd run his own restaurant for years, but had wanted a career change. The reality of teaching wasn't what he'd expected: the school was chaotic, the headteacher ineffective, and staff left virtually every term. He was in danger of failing his induction year and he was considering a return to catering.

I liked him instantly, and I felt he hadn't been given a fair chance. I had a vacancy for September, and on the spur of the moment I offered it to him. The LEA's Human Resources Department would have been appalled – appointing a teacher now involves a 28-stage process – but sod it, I had a gut feeling about this.

Alex was a success from the moment he walked into our school. An incredibly hard worker, he gained the affection of the children within days. When he asked me how often I'd like to see his planning, he was astonished when I said I didn't want to see it at all. His previous senior managers, none of whom ever went near a classroom, had marked his planning with detailed and often vitriolic comments.

I explained that I'd pop into his classroom regularly for a while and join in with a lesson or two. I'd know instantly if things weren't working well – and if they weren't, there was much friendly expertise in the school that could help him.

By the time two years had passed, he was thoroughly involved with every aspect of the school, and loving it. He organized a link with a poor school in Gambia, and his children designed and organized a series of playground sideshows to raise money. It was a tremendous success – the most popular event being Alex strapped in a chair, with children paying 10p and lining up to squash a shaving-foam pie on his head.

Like all great teachers, he had a delightful sense of humour. While explaining to an inspector that he was a little tired because his son had recently been born, she asked if it had affected his performance. 'Well,' he said, 'my wife hasn't complained yet ...'

What especially pleased me was the time he was willing to give to his children. Once, as Mason talked constantly at him during lunch, I suggested he should give Alex a little peace. 'Nah', said Mason, grinning affectionately. "E don't deserve it.' Mason was an extremely challenging boy, his home life was grim, and his father hardly an ideal role model. But Alex was.

When I started an after-school table tennis club, I discovered that Alex was also a good player, and we began regular Friday matches after the children had finished. Then we'd sit and chat about the week. Performance management as it should be done! I was really looking forward to seeing what he could do with a different year group in September.

And then, just before half term, he told me he'd be leaving in the summer. His wife, a barrister, gets much of her work in Kent, his son starts school shortly, and a house had become available. He was very sad to be going, but it seemed a timely move.

Alex has given a great deal to my school. What have I given him? Well, his confidence, and the freedom to discover teaching's pleasures. He'll make a cracking deputy head very soon.

And in September I shall miss him very much.

May

Forty-eight
Questions! Eighty-three pointless questions!

Big Brother has arrived. I have proof.

During a typical school year, Secretary Sandra and I fill in a variety of forms for a range of audiences. A few are useful. Most aren't. The school 'Self Evaluation Form', for example, which, despite what anybody tells you, is really for Ofsted so that inspectors from miles away have a vague idea of what's happening in your school before they spend two days rummaging around it. Even then, they often get it wrong.

But the forms that really annoy me usually emanate from the Department for Education. The PLASC, for example. No, I can't remember what the acronym stands for either, but it's a sort of massive school census that began life at a reasonable length some years ago and has expanded rapidly ever since. And now it's required three times a year.

I can only assume the government suits have no idea what life is like in a primary school. They seem to think people in the school office are constantly looking for something to do, their role being to fill the void.

The form that arrived this week, however, really takes the biscuit. It's called the School Workforce Census and it bounced into school via the local authority. When she saw it, Secretary Sandra's mouth dropped open in astonishment. Ten screens – 83 questions in all – have to be completed for every adult working in the building. You can't duplicate information from one person's file to another, either. It would be helpful, for example, to call up the screens for your male staff and enter 'Mr' in them all at the click of a button. But no, you have to do them one at a time.

Then you stare at the questions in disbelief. The first screen asks for a person's initials, surname, salutation, known name, legal surname, maiden name, initials and second name. Then their address, email, home phone, mobile, passport, nationality, ethnicity, mother tongue, religion, disability, CRB, ID check, references … you name it, it's in there, everything apart from the colour of their knickers. I calculated it would take Sandra two days just to fill in one of these forms, even if she had the time, which she hasn't.

Gender is next. Is the person male, female, or – you're not going to believe this – is their gender 'not known'. Okay, call me naive, but I haven't met too many people who aren't sure of their gender. What are they supposed to do, slip behind the piano and check?

And then – hand on heart, I'm not making this up – there are questions about your car. Why on earth would the government want to know the make of teachers' cars? And not only the make; they want the licence plate number and the colour as well. I suppose they wouldn't be – surely not – intending to flog all this information to marketing consultants, would they?

Irritated, I phoned an LEA statistics officer. No, he didn't know why they wanted car colours either, and he said we needn't bother filling that bit in. But that isn't the point. Why is the question included? In fact, I haven't a clue why the Department needs most of the information on this form, particularly since much of it is already held in staff confidential files. I told the officer I had no intention of asking Sandra to waste her time unless the Department of Education sent me a comprehensive letter of explanation.

And then I had an idea. We'd fill them in, but we'd say every teacher owns a Porsche, the average age of the staff is 105, everybody's religion is Russian Orthodox and the teachers only have qualifications in raffia-work, Plasticine and Morris dancing.

And we'll see what they make of that.

Forty-nine
Tree tale that gave me the pip

Sometimes I think school is the last bastion of honesty and integrity. Right from their Nursery age, like good parents we encourage our children to become caring, thinking human beings, with a strong sense of social responsibility.

These days, it's pretty hard. I'd hate to be a secondary school teacher in a citizenship lesson, attempting to persuade a class of teenagers that our democratically elected leaders had moral integrity. Like most of the population, I feel intense anger about some of the people who lead us.

And call me over-sensitive, but I felt this year's Year 6 SATs comprehension test didn't help. The booklet the children had to read was about a little boy called Norman, who'd argued with his parents and taken himself off to live in a tree house at the end of his garden. The booklet consisted of letters written to Norman by family and friends. There are indications that he wrote back, so presumably he'd stormed up the tree complete with a pad of Basildon Bond and a fistful of Biros.

The first letters are from his mum and dad. Dad wishes him all the best for his exciting new life among the branches, and understands that his decision to leave the family is a serious one. Mum is grateful to him for explaining all the things she and dad got wrong, and says his advice is very helpful.

Good bit of middle class psychology here. Pander to your child's every whim, pretend he's a miniature adult instead of a little boy – and, get this – even allow him to lug a television up the tree. A good job health and safety officers weren't in the neighbourhood, although they would presumably reassure Norm that he wasn't in danger of electrocution, since electricity isn't normally found up trees. If things go on like this, though, I've a feeling Supernanny might be on the way ...

Then comes a sour little note from his sister. She's nicked his bedroom! Ha ha, she says, mum and dad said I could have it. This is followed by a formal letter from his class teacher, undoubtedly taking time out in the evening from targeting and tracking, to advise him on the life skills he'll need in his leafy retreat. It seems his parents popped in to see her, explaining that Norman wouldn't be coming to school anymore because he was now living in a tree. Mind you, perhaps that's not so strange. A parent once came to see me, asking if I could have a word with Andrew because he kept climbing into wheelie bins.

Turn the page and we meet Grandma, in both words and pictures because there's a photo with her letter. And a miserable old harridan she looks, too. She witters on about how lonely she is, how her grandchildren don't visit often enough, and how Norman's father hasn't written to her for ages. Frankly, if she was coming for lunch I'd be up there with Norman. She's certainly unlike any grandparent I've ever known. I'd always thought grandparents were overgenerous, cuddly, and adored by their grandchildren.

Still, Norm has one good friend. Alfred writes and says how totally cool living up a tree is, because he won't have to wash, or to brush his teeth. Presumably he doesn't realize he'll have to keep his distance after a couple of weeks, because his mate Norm will soon stink like a polecat. And then he says, 'Oh, by the way. Can I have your bike?' What a charming friend.

It all ends well. Mr Precocious comes down from his tree because – wait for it – he's won a competition about solving the world's problems and he's off to meet the President of the USA. Before he does that, let's hope he gets sent to bed with a severe wigging and no supper!

Fifty
An old boy with distinction

It's nice when children come back during the year to see you.

Usually, Year 6 children visit as soon as they've started secondary school, because they're keen to show off their smart new uniforms and complicated timetables. Then they quickly settle into new routines, and you only see them when there's no school and they're at a loose end, or if they're not settling very happily into their new surroundings.

Some appear at your door in their late teens. They'll tell you proudly that they're training, or studying at college. They remember their primary school with pleasure and want you to know they're doing well. It's gratifying – and occasionally it's surprising, especially when a youngster visits who spent most of his primary years being a thorough pain in the neck.

Muhammed was such a child. He was in his final year when I joined the school as headteacher, and I learned that he'd been very difficult in Year 5. I was warned that I'd probably have to exclude him in his final year.

Undoubtedly he could be charming. He was the first child I encountered when I arrived at Comber Grove, because he was always the first to arrive in the playground each morning. He offered to carry my bags upstairs, and when we reached my office his eyes darted quickly around the room. I had the impression, even then, that half an hour later he could have drawn me an accurate map of everything it contained.

Within days, I discovered that nothing was safe when he was in the vicinity unless it was nailed down. But catching him was impossible. I also found that he could irritate his classmates with consummate skill, causing arguments that degenerated into utter chaos – at which point, like Macavity, Muhammed wasn't there.

But we had to get through the year, and I suggested giving him a main part in my Christmas play. This occupied him for several hours a week, to his teacher's delight, but brought me undeniable grief. Muhammed constantly re-wrote his part, demanding that other cast members keep up with his changes and giving them a tongue lashing if they didn't.

He'd take himself off to the stockroom and use copious amounts of expensive card to create intricate props he'd designed. He'd persuade teaching assistants I'd said he could stay in at lunchtime to rehearse – and chocolate bars would suddenly disappear from lunchboxes. Ultimately, the rest of the cast rebelled and said they didn't want to be in the play until I'd sorted Muhammed out.

Then, at hometime one freezing winter day, my car keys disappeared. I'd left them on my table while I fetched my coat, and I searched everywhere, until a cleaner said she'd seen Muhammed go into my room.

I rushed downstairs and caught him by the door, asking if he'd seen my keys. He looked surprised and hurt, offering to turn out his pockets. Two weeks later, he put his head round my door, grinned, and jingled a bunch of car keys. 'Are these yours, sir?' he asked innocently. 'I found them in the road.'

Shortly afterwards, Muhammed was sent to the library to work. A special needs group was also in the room, reading with a teacher. At lunch time, the teacher popped out to the shop and realized her credit cards were missing from her bag. This time I told Muhammed I'd have to search him, but he raised no objection, merely expressing his sympathy for the teacher's loss and offering to help look.

Somehow, we reached the end of the year, and Muhammed moved on. Then, seven years later, a smart young man appeared in the corridor. It was Muhammed, and he wanted me to know how well he was doing. He'd almost finished his business studies and was going into partnership with a friend. Pleased to know things were going well, I invited him to say hello to the teachers he knew.

Four years later, he appeared again, in a smart suit and carrying a very expensive briefcase. His business was successful, he was marrying soon, and he hoped he could put his children in our school as it had given him – I had difficulty keeping a straight face – such a good start in life. Once again I expressed pleasure at how things had turned out …

… Until, thumbing through the pages of an evening paper a year later, I stopped at a photograph of a young man wanted for a string of daring robberies from hotels in one of London's smartest districts. Always immaculately dressed, said the headline, and carrying an expensive briefcase …

Fifty-one
Life is a rollercoaster ride

I've always enjoyed taking school assemblies.

Sure, you can chat about healthy eating, or why it's daft to smoke, but you can also introduce your own interests. During the past year I've told the children how I became a writer, how magicians cut people in half, how I taught myself the banjo, how I sprayed a door on my classic MG, and how I built a little cinema in my loft. My message is simple. Life is a lot more interesting than watching television or fiddling with a PlayStation.

Occasionally, something I've demonstrated really fires them up and they talk about it for days. My rollercoaster Assembly, for example. I've loved rollercoasters since I was thirteen, and I'd recently been with my family to Florida, riding some of the tallest and most exciting in the world. In Assembly, I demonstrated how they'd evolved over the last 50 years – stacks of science here. I held up large, colourful photos of vertical-drop coasters, wooden coasters, looping coasters. I explained acceleration speeds and braking technology.

Then a little history – and screams of delight – when I ran an old Super 8 film taken from the front car of a Big Dipper at Blackpool. And finally, by swinging a bucket half full of water in a complete circle, I showed how centrifugal force helps hold riders in the car, even when they're upside down. The children were astonished when the water didn't come out, and Alison stayed behind after Assembly, looking at the bucket thoughtfully. 'Could I have a go at that?' she asked. 'It takes a bit of practice', I said. 'Come and see me tomorrow when I've time to show you.'

Throughout the day I was stopped by children asking how I'd done 'that magic trick with the bucket and water'. 'It wasn't a trick', I'd say. 'It was centrifugal force – I explained it to you in Assembly.' 'Yes,' they'd say, 'but how did you do that trick with the bucket and water?'

On Wednesday at playtime, Alison knocked on my door. Would it be okay for her to have a go if she went to the Nursery and borrowed one of their little buckets? I explained that the Nursery was closed for the day, and that she should try tomorrow. I was sure she'd forget – and that would save our tiniest children from being showered with water.

On Thursday, two things happened. In the morning, two Infants children rushed excitedly into my room brandishing corrugated paper plates and pieces of wood. 'We've wrote a roller coaster rap!' they said, and proceeded to dance around my room, singing the words and working up a lively rhythm with their plates and scrapers. Secretary Sandra peered round the door, scratched her head, and disappeared again.

Then, in the afternoon, David came to see me. He'd gone home after my Assembly, seen his dad painting the ceiling, and offered to show him a clever trick with the contents of the paint kettle. Dad, fearing for his carpet, informed his son that if he went within a metre of the kettle he'd emulsion his head.

Then, on Friday, Alison was back – with a bucket from the Nursery. Never one to rain on the bonfire of enthusiasm, I stood her in the middle of my room, moved everything out of the way, put some water in her bucket, and told her to have a go. Taking a deep breath, she swung the bucket upwards, took fright, and showered herself with water.

Next week in Assembly, I'm going for the easy option. I'll just tell the children why they shouldn't lock each other in the toilets.

Fifty-two
Playground spy follows the clues

At 3.15 p.m., I stand at the top of the staircase leading to the playground, and I say goodnight to each child. Behind me is a window, and I can look down and watch the children greet their parents, sometimes in an unexpected manner. Sadie, for example, is a charming, well behaved child in class, and I watched her skip out of school and ask her mum for an ice cream. Her mother refused, whereupon Sadie gave her a violent kick on the shin.

On another occasion, I could hear Mrs Elton asking Andrew why he hadn't brought his reading book down. She asked him to fetch it, and he refused. She asked again – firmly. Andrew promptly sat down and refused to move. Mrs Elton looked at him for a moment, and then sat beside him, saying they needed to discuss the matter. The fact that the playground was very wet from the heavy rain earlier in the afternoon didn't seem to bother either of them, but I couldn't help wondering which of the two was in charge.

It's interesting to see how parents deal with petulance. Often, those who can't cope with the behaviour of their own children give class teachers the most grief. Defending a child's behaviour seems an attempt to gain respect, and this sometimes leads to odd conversations, like the one I had with Charlie's mum. Charlie was difficult at home. Dad had left, and mum was struggling. But, proud and defiant, she defended his every action. She also had trouble prising him out of bed, and it was unusual to see him in school before 10.30.

Exasperated, I wrote a letter explaining her legal obligation to get her son in by nine. After school, she came striding down the corridor, brandishing my letter in the air. 'Are you aware', she roared, 'it's a proven fact that children who are late for school are more successful in later life?' I said I'd willingly check her assertion, but in the meantime could she just stick to the law and get her son to school on time?

The incident involving Jamoy took some beating. His teacher had gone to the classroom at breaktime to fetch her handbag, and she found Jamoy's hand deep inside it. A five-pound note was in his other hand. His mother was telephoned, and after school she appeared in my office, demanding to speak to me. Jamoy, it seemed, was not guilty. The class teacher explained that she'd actually caught Jamoy with his hand in her bag. 'Well, my boy has just told me he didn't do it', she said. 'And that's good enough for me.' No doubt his mother will eventually tell the judge that her son only robbed the safe because he liked playing with combination numbers.

But sometimes my conversations with parents are delightfully Pinteresque. I run a table tennis club for the older children after school on Fridays, and Mrs Anderson asked me how Tom could get to play. I explained that I could only take eight children, so it was first come first served, and I operated on a rota basis, one week Year 6, the next Year 5. I explained that he needed to sign up on a Monday.

'So table tennis is on Mondays?'

'No, it's on Fridays. But children need to sign up on Mondays.'

'So if he signs up next Monday, he can play?'

'No, because it's Year 6 next week.'

'So Year 6 play on a Monday?'

'No, they play on Fridays.'

'So what do they play on Mondays?'

Eventually, I thought I'd got through. Until I found Tom waiting in the hall after school on Wednesday.

'What time's table tennis?' he asked.

Fifty-three
Oh no! Someone's watching our performance again!

It seems we can't go for more than a month without another performance management document landing on our desks. Usually, it says the rules have changed because a working party has found the last working party's decisions unworkable. Invariably, the new model means more work.

But the circular that arrived last week had me chuckling into my morning coffee, and for a moment or two I thought that somebody with a wry sense of humour in the ivory towers of the LEA had created it to lighten my day. But no, as I read further, I realized it was deadly serious. It described the procedural changes in performance management to be made this year.

On the front page, there was a photograph of two people, a teacher and a reviewer, poring over the teacher's performance management document. This wasn't a few sheets of paper, though. It was an entire roll of the stuff. It looked as if the teacher had spent the whole summer holiday scribbling her life story on a roll of anaglypta. Since they were of similar ages, and didn't have leather patches on their sleeves or paint blobs on their clothing, it was also pretty difficult to tell which one was the teacher.

Page 2 gave details of a course designed to update heads on current requirements, and I quote the opening sentence in full, simply because I defy you to remain awake by the end it …

> The new performance management regulations require reviewers to align school development priorities with professional development needs, demanding of reviewers a thorough understanding of the teacher's standards and progression possibilities and the ability to set objectives producing outcomes in the form of evidence upon which the overall performance of the teacher will be judged.

Then we're told the course is being run by a 'consultant experienced in performance management'. It doesn't mention whether he actually knows anything about schools. Or teaching.

The notion of performance management leaves me cold. If senior managers are properly in touch with the staff and their needs, I see no purpose in it. I have 40 adults working in my school, all at different stages of their lives and careers. Some are perfectly content to do what they're doing, some are interested in promotion, some want to further their careers in other ways. If a teacher or teaching assistant wants to sit and chat about their career with me for an hour after school, my door is always open and I'm always available.

If I think somebody should be considering a move upwards, I'll seek them out and talk about it. I'll know if a teacher is having problems, or needs practical support, because I visit classrooms often and I'm interested in what's going on. But I'm not at all interested in putting lots of writing on bits of paper to justify myself.

Frankly, I don't know of any good, effective school that undertakes performance management exactly as it is supposed to be done. It's a massive amount of work, sorting staff into groups, with harassed team leaders trying to find time to interview them all when their time would be better spent organizing their classrooms or teaching the children. Naturally, there's plenty of form filling, and then follow-up meetings to check if 'targets' have been achieved.

Before you know it, a new year arrives, and the whole ridiculous cycle starts again. The benefits? Well, if you're a senior manager who doesn't like children, the workload is a good way of avoiding them. And Ofsted inspectors will pat you on the back when they see the size of your file, because that's what they care about.

Parkinson's Law was never more prevalent. Mr P must be chuckling in his grave.

June

Fifty-four
Boys will be boys, unless they are buses

I watched '*Goodbye Mr Chips*' again last night.

In the poignant last scene, Chips lies in bed, about to go to that great classroom in the sky. 'Shame he never had any children of his own', another teacher says softly. 'No children?' overhears Chips. 'I'm a teacher – I've had thousands of children …'

This is the fascinating thing about the teaching profession. All those children. All different, all so interesting.

Like Robert. When he joined us in Year 2, his mother hadn't mentioned he was autistic, but all those years ago autism went almost unrecognized in schools. Talking about dinosaurs in Robert's first Assembly, I mispronounced 'diplodocus'. Up piped a loud voice. 'It's not docus, as in crocus. It's od, as in plod. The diplodocus is one of the longest and most interesting dinosaurs from the Jurassic period. The reptile attained lengths up to 80 feet and had a long neck, body and flexible tail …' I hadn't known about his passion for dinosaurs, and he continued for a full two minutes. The other children stared, mouths agape.

Frankie was another unforgettable child, although he wasn't autistic. He simply had an all-enveloping passion for buses. He'd also joined us from elsewhere, and it was a fortnight before I met him properly. I was in the playground, chatting to his teacher, when he wandered up to us.

'Shall I do a bus, Miss?' he asked. Seeing my baffled expression, his teacher smiled. 'Frankie's my very own bus service', she said. 'Shut your eyes and listen.'

He launched into an impression of a bus in motion, with gear changes, stops and starts, and hissing air brakes. It sounded just like the real thing.

'What bus was that?' he asked, expecting us to know. 'I reckon it's a number 53', said his teacher. 'Of course it's not!' he replied indignantly. 'It's a Bendy Bus. *This* is a 53 …' He embarked on a second impression, which sounded very different.

By half term, we'd adapted to his quirkiness. Each day, I stand on the staircase and chat to the children as they pass me after playtime, and one morning Frankie decided to play bus conductor, announcing the stop we had reached.

'This is East Dulwich. Along that corridor is Peckham Rye. If we go up another flight we'll be in Forest Hill. Ask Miss if you can look at my maps.'

I discovered that Frankie had drawn elaborate maps of the school, re-creating the building as a large chunk of south-east London. Bus routes were marked with coloured lines and stops were marked at intervals. To catch the P13 to Streatham, also known as the school dinner hall, you had to wait outside Class 9, where buses should appear at ten minute intervals if they were on schedule.

Frankie could give any school activity a transport slant. On an outing, while other boys sat assessing the contents of their packed lunches, Frankie unfolded a huge bus map, laid it out on an empty seat, and carefully studied the route they were taking. I was relieved he wasn't sitting directly behind the coach driver, outlining alternatives and faster ways to get there.

His class teacher, from South Africa, was initially unfamiliar with London, but after teaching Frankie for two years she felt that she could travel anywhere by bus. Frankie loved them, studied them incessantly, and by now has undoubtedly found a career with them.

Soon after he'd left us for secondary school, I met him with his mother in a shop, miles from where he lived. 'You're a long way from home', I said. 'How did you get here?'

'Dear God, please don't ask him that', his mother said. 'We'll be here all morning.'

Fifty-five
Safeguards strike fear into our families

One of our fathers has three children, and a good relationship with us. While he was unemployed, he enjoyed bringing his three children to school each morning. But he recently secured short-term work and now gets up very early, before his children are awake. He returns late in the evening to his cramped flat in a high-rise block. He loves his children, but he and his wife find them increasingly difficult to control. There's little space for play, and they are particularly boisterous at bedtime.

Because he is tired after long working hours, dad's patience has been on a knife-edge. After warning the oldest child about his behaviour, he lost his temper and struck him with a stick. The child's teacher noticed the mark and the child explained – after a little hesitation – what had happened, but said his father has never done anything like this before.

Faced with a situation like this, what should a headteacher do? My inclination would be to meet the parents and discuss ways the children might be occupied more effectively. I'd also want to explain how school might help and support the situation. But I'd make it clear that using a stick is illegal, and that I'd take the matter further if it happened again. In this way, I'd hopefully retain their trust and respect, while issuing a warning that I hoped they'd heed.

In fact, I can't do any of that. If a child reports being struck, current safeguarding rules insist I must complete and email a referral to Social Services immediately.

An instant decision will be made, usually meaning a visit, at school, from a Social Services worker and a police officer. I will be required to keep the child separated from the parents after school until they arrive. They will interview the child, talk to the parents at length, and make a decision on whether it is safe for the child to go home. If necessary, they will arrange for a doctor to examine the child and personally escort them to the surgery. A file will be opened on the family and a Common Assessment Form started, so that every involved professional can update and share information.

At least, that's the theory. But, like everything to do with human beings, it never works out that neatly.

In a recent case I dealt with, the police officer and social worker didn't arrive until well after the end of the school day. The mother couldn't understand why she wasn't allowed to see her child, and she raised her voice in the corridor, to the consternation of other parents and children. She telephoned the father, who demanded the child be allowed home. Two of my teachers occupied the child, but she quickly became distressed and bewildered.

When the police officer and social worker arrived, they disagreed about the procedure they should adopt, which further complicated matters. By the time the child was taken to a doctor, two hours had passed.

Eventually, since the facts seemed different from the way they'd been presented by the child, she was allowed to go home, and it was decided no follow-up was needed. The parents' relationship with each other, and with the school, dipped alarmingly, and took a long time to repair. The father suddenly found he couldn't get a job because, mistakenly, he'd acquired a criminal record. We'd started a Common Assessment Form, but nobody else had bothered to add any information.

The rapidly increasing volume of referrals these days usually causes Social Services, understandably, to request additional information before deciding whether to take action. The police tell us this is irrelevant; a child being struck with an implement should be all that is needed to trigger total Social Services and police involvement.

To me, this misses the heart of the matter. As a result of high-profile cases in the media, Social Services are hounded and under pressure as never before. But a school knows its families well, and is in a unique position to judge how matters should proceed, and to ring alarm bells if necessary.

Frankly, if we're not careful, increasingly complex safeguarding regulations are going to make things a whole lot worse, not better.

Fifty-six
A dab hand at pigeon prodding

There's nothing more pleasant than hearing wood pigeons cooing in the countryside on a warm, fresh summer morning. But town pigeons, well, they're another kettle of feathers altogether.

My school is in a densely populated area, and pigeons have always been a problem. They stroll nonchalantly into the playground, heads bobbing away, hunting for food scraps. Before we became an accredited healthy school, we sold breaktime biscuits and the pigeons scrabbled for crumbs in the playground, calling their mates to join in with the feast.

Pigeons might not be very bright, but they soon become bold. Once the playground scraps had been swallowed, a few wandered into the building searching for more, and then couldn't find their way out again. When children discovered a pigeon in school, some, unsurprisingly, were frightened. Others wanted to stroke them. A few chased them up the corridor, causing the birds to make rapid bowel evacuations on the floor. Or, even worse, in mid-air.

Then the days of increased school security arrived, and doors were no longer left open. But teachers sometimes inadvertently left classroom windows open at hometime, and pigeons started flying through those instead. Other than having an Ofsted inspector in your classroom, there's nothing more disconcerting than sitting your children down while you call the register, and then finding a pigeon joining in from its perch on a high window ledge.

Hunting through my 'All You Need To Know About Being A Headteacher' manual, I could find nothing relating to 'pigeons, removal of', but fortunately Premises Officer Dave had been working away at the problem. He'd bought a telescopic metal pole, and screwed what looked like a fisherman's net to one end of it and a brush to the other. The brush end soon proved useful when a cleaner was startled by a noise coming from a staircase radiator. A pigeon had come in the window, perched on the radiator for warmth, and then fallen behind it, where it sat there flapping its wings in fright – until Dave managed to give it a releasing shove with his brush and trap it with his net. Armed with a couple of these tools, we felt equipped to tackle any avian intruder.

And then things suddenly turned serious.

While sweeping the playground first thing in the morning, Dave noticed three pigeons flying through a skylight into the loft area of the building. Dave rarely goes into the loft. Provided the water tanks aren't leaking, it's not a place you want to spend much time in, but he thought it best to climb up and have a peep.

His eyes opened wide with horror. Grilles at both ends of the loft had broken away, the whole area was thickly covered in white bird droppings, adult birds were careering to and fro around the roof beams, eggs were nestling in the rafters, and recently hatched youngsters blinked happily at him in the sunlight. Hurrying back down the ladder, Dave immediately sent for assistance.

When the pest control specialists arrived, it took the best part of a week to remove the eggs, clean the worst of the mess, seal the skylights with new mesh and fix pigeon-resistant spikes to the roof. Had we not called them, they said, the roof timbers would eventually have rotted and possibly caused a classroom ceiling to collapse. A sigh of relief and £2,000 later, we thought the problem had been solved.

Until Monday morning, when a teacher on the top floor discovered four pigeons in her classroom. They'd been hovering all weekend, annoyed they couldn't get into the loft. Presumably they couldn't believe their luck when they found an open window that Dave hadn't noticed.

Hopefully, they'll soon tire of trying and move somewhere else. I'll be keeping the spikes, though. Just in case any Ofsted inspectors are trying to land . . .

Fifty-seven
The lift that wouldn't

Summer approaching, and it's time for School Journeys. Considering teachers spend anything up to a fortnight on these Journeys looking after the children, I'm always amazed by how few parents say thank you when they collect their children afterwards. But it's worse when parents don't collect their children at all ...

Daniel was such a child. I waited with the parents as the coach arrived and suitcases were unloaded. Within 15 minutes, everyone had gone. Except Daniel, who stood beside his large, tatty case, looking thoroughly miserable. His mother was supposed to be picking him up, he said. Possibly. Or maybe it was his sister, if she could get time off work. He couldn't remember. I reassured him, saying his mother had probably been delayed.

Another half hour passed, and my deputy tried to phone his mother. The line had been cut off. Nothing for it but to wait with Daniel a bit longer.

After another hour, we decided to see if a neighbour would look after him. Since his case looked as if it might empty its contents all over the pavement if we lifted it, we tied a belt round it and hurried through the pouring rain and into the lift at Daniel's block of flats, as we didn't fancy hauling the case up the stairs. The lift was full of graffiti, and there was a puddle on the floor that smelt of pee. The three of us huddled into the least rubbish-strewn corner. 'It's always like this, Miss', said Daniel resignedly. 'And it often breaks down.'

Which it did, 30 seconds later. Between floors. 'Don't worry, I know how to get it going again', said Daniel. He removed his shoe and whacked the control panel. The lift juddered, but didn't budge. 'It sometimes works if you jump up and down', he said.

Feeling foolish, we bounced around for a minute or two. Still no movement. 'I'll try the alarm button', I said. 'It's broken', said Daniel. 'Someone mucked about with the wires.'

Small, confined spaces aren't really my thing, and I began to feel uneasy. As there seemed nothing for it but to summon assistance, my deputy and I shouted 'Help!' as loudly as we could. Daniel found this very amusing, and joined in with enthusiasm. Moments later, a door some distance away opened and a voice called 'Are you stuck in the lift?'

We certainly were, I said, and we'd be everlastingly grateful if someone could help us to become unstuck. A muttering from above – and then a child's voice said 'Mum, it sounds like Mr Kent!' Moments later, an older voice called out. 'This is Jodie's Mum. That's not you down there, Mr Kent, is it?' 'I'm afraid so,' I called, 'and Mrs Matthews is stuck in here with me.' 'And me, I'm stuck too', shouted Daniel, enjoying this very much.

Other doors opened and there were fascinated murmurs as it became known that the leadership team of the local primary school was stuck halfway up a lift shaft. 'Don't worry, Sir,' shouted Jodie, 'my brother's got a spanner.' 'That won't work', said her mother. 'I'll ring the fire brigade, Mr Kent. Just hold on till they get here.' Funny how, at times like this, you always find yourself dying to go to the toilet.

'We might be here hours', said Daniel. 'Shall I show you a magic trick?'

After what seemed an eternity, Jodie's mother called again. 'My neighbour's home', she said. 'He's got an idea...' A male voice said he'd been caught in this bleedin' lift more times than he'd had hot dinners, and that if we distributed our weight around and pushed the button hard, it would probably start.

The relief when it did was overwhelming. It clattered to the top floor, the doors opened, and there stood the neighbour holding the biggest screwdriver we'd ever seen. 'Sometimes the doors don't open', he said. 'My wife keeps this handy...'

As we hurried back to school, we heard the fire engine in the distance. We didn't wait around to explain. Daniel would've done that on our behalf: the perfect end to his School Journey ...

Fifty-eight
Vicki given the freedom to breathe

At the moment, I'm compiling the end-of-year report on Vicki, the newly qualified teacher who joined us last September.

I like having NQTs on the staff. I love the freshness and enthusiasm they bring to the job, although I'm astonished at how much bureaucratic baggage they have to handle these days.

It was very different, back in the sixties, when I was given my first job. I visited the school during the summer term, eager-eyed and raring to inspire the young. I looked forward to a friendly interview with the headteacher and a rundown on what I'd be expected to do.

I knocked on his door, pushed it open, and interrupted him furtively downing a bottle of school milk intended for the children. Embarrassed, he pumped my hand briefly, took me to the classroom that would be mine in September, and told me I'd find textbooks in the cupboard, plus pencils, a blackboard rubber and a box of chalk. If I wanted exercise books for the children, I'd have to see Mrs Floyd in September, but only on a Monday, mind, because Mondays were her stock days.

And that was that. But after a hesitant start and a steep learning curve, I had a wonderful year, and so, I think, did my children. Teaching techniques influenced by the Plowden Report, whereby teachers could more or less decide their own curriculum, were in full force, and the freedom I had was exhilarating.

When there was something I couldn't do, I sought help. And I studied how the best teachers organized their rooms and their lessons. Unlike today, non-contact time didn't exist; I often did two playground duties and a lunchtime duty on the same day, but at least nobody looked over my shoulder and monitored me every five minutes.

And that's one of education's troubles these days, I think. Undoubtedly, much has improved since my classroom teaching days, but the staggering workload heaped on a trainee teacher's shoulders makes me wonder how NQTs get through it, especially those, like Vicki, who have children of their own. If the training doesn't cripple them, once they arrive in the classroom they're presented with the induction regulations and an enormous folder of stuff at the first meeting with their LEA.

There are 41 – yes, 41 – core standards to be mastered, such as 'showing a commitment to ensure children reach their full potential', and the necessity for 'creating a safe learning environment'. I bet that last one surprised you. Who'd have thought that children should be educated in a safe environment?

Then there'll be classroom observations by senior staff, objectives for meeting core standards, half-termly progress reviews, assessment meetings ...

Which brings me back to my opening sentence, because this report is about all I do. Though, before you throw up your hands in horror, let me qualify that. An NQT at my school is assigned a mentor, a thoroughly experienced, friendly colleague who meets the newcomer regularly. Not to talk about standards, targets, or all the other mind-numbing paraphernalia, but to chat through issues, problems, classroom organization. I pop into the teacher's classroom frequently, to see how things are going. Every member of my staff will offer the NQT day-to-day encouragement.

But most importantly, the new teacher will be given the space to breathe. Invariably, after a very short time, she'll be the first at school in the mornings, loaded down with exciting bits and pieces, and she'll often be the last to leave. Once that stage is reached, she's well on her way, and if she needs help or guidance she'll ask for it.

It worked well for me 40 years ago, and NQTs still come to me at the end of their induction year to say thank you – for leaving them alone!

July

Fifty-nine
Let loose in the corridors of power

I'm off on a trip to the Houses of Parliament with Year 6. I've been a Londoner all my life but I've never done the tour, so it's an ideal opportunity.

The children get into pairs and we file to the bus stop. It's a squeeze, but we're all able to get on the same bus, spreading along its length. Almost immediately, Sadie feels sick, and I watch a couple of passengers shift cautiously. Fortunately, she's not in my bit of the bus, and one of the teachers is fully equipped with plastic bags. She tells Sadie to breathe deeply and look straight ahead.

The bus trip is short, Sadie's fine, and soon we're walking along Horse Guard's Parade and into St James's Park. It's a glorious morning, and I think how lucky the ducks are. A beautiful park, a rippling pond to swim on, plenty of foliage, and passers-by with lots of bread.

Though it's relatively early, the teachers decide we should have lunch now, rather than carry bags around Westminster Palace. The children sit on the grass and unpack their lunches. Michael doesn't have one, because his mother couldn't be bothered. I'd anticipated this, and before coming out I'd nipped into the kitchen and asked our Cook if she'd prepare some salad rolls – one for me and one for Michael. She's included yoghurts and bananas, so Michael is well fed. He likes the yoghurt but rejects the banana, offering it to an inquisitive squirrel instead.

Olamide has cake in his packed lunch. Not a slice, mind; an entire cake. Similarly, Yassim has a large packet of custard creams. I wonder what their mothers were thinking, and then realize they probably gave their offspring money to buy their own packed lunch. Neither parent seems to be enthusiastically supporting our anti-obesity drive.

It's time to move on, and we arrive at Security. Michael asks me if the policemen will be carrying Kalashnikovs, and I say probably not. The children are intrigued to find their photos need to be taken and our belongings passed through scanners. My tray of belongings sets off the buzzer, and I realize there's a metal spoon in my bag. The

Cook had slipped it in so that I'd have something to eat my yoghurt with.

We enter the palace and the classes break into groups and go off with the guides we've booked. The guide escorting my class is terrific and gives the impression we're the first party he's ever shown around, answering the children's questions skilfully at just the right level.

He throws in fascinating titbits, pointing out the wall concealing the royal toilet in the Queen's Room, plumbed in Queen Victoria's time while the sewers were being built. 'Before that,' he says, 'the waste would go into the Thames and smell pretty grim on the hot summer days. That's why MPs needed long holidays.' 'Well it don't smell now,' William points out, 'but they still have long holidays.'

Our guide falters only once. We sit on benches opposite shelves of large red tomes, and he fetches one down, explaining that this is Hansard, and everything said in parliament is recorded in these big red books. He asks for questions and Lyndon raises his hand. 'What are those big red books?' he asks. For a moment our guide thinks Lyndon is being cheeky, but then, he's not familiar with Lyndon's attention span.

We pass through the debating chamber and Amid shows concern at the damage Black Rod is doing to the door by hammering on it. A bit of wood filler would sort that out, he reckons. At the end of the tour we reach the bookstall and Sarah discovers the free brochures and booklets. Word spreads and soon every child has an armful. I think of the burden on our taxes.

But as we board the bus for school, I realize how much I've enjoyed the morning. I must get out more. And there's a bonus: it seems I've missed Braidon's mum, who was up complaining yet again ...

Sixty
Music on a rising scale

I've realized a 25-year-old dream …

I believe music is a vital ingredient of the primary curriculum, though when I joined Comber Grove in the early eighties there wasn't much of it going on. Five guitars – two of them broken and one too large for a primary child – a handful of percussion instruments and a box of recorders was about the sum of it, plus a bit of singing now and again. Boys in Years 5 and 6 didn't join in, though. It wasn't considered cool when you were at the top of the school.

Where to start? Well, I had time in those days, because headteachers didn't have to spend hours filling in silly forms and gathering data. I could throw myself wholeheartedly into my new job. Since I played guitar, the first step was to form a guitar group, and I asked the local music store if I could have some discount if I ordered more than one instrument. When I said I wanted 25, he was my friend for life … and I started virtually all of Year 3 on weekly lessons. Within a short time, they could play half a dozen tunes. They'd pluck the notes, I'd pick the chords, and they made an impressive debut one morning in Assembly.

Soon we'd added recorder groups and tuned percussion, and, together with a talented and musical member of staff, I formed a choir. No problem in getting girls to join, but when the boys saw that singing could actually be fun, and that even with my cracked voice I was willing to have a go, our choir expanded rapidly, though the quality was questionable for a while.

But we'd still only achieved what most primary schools achieve. Now I wanted something more challenging, and I bought six second-hand brass instruments. I couldn't teach brass … but I knew a man who could. Joe, an orchestral player, had taught brass at the school where I'd been deputy head, and he agreed to join me. By Christmas, his little band was playing Jingle Bells in the end-of-term school concert.

Around this time, my friendly music shopkeeper had some violins for sale. They weren't in great condition, he said, but I could have them for a song, and he knew somebody who had a spare hour on Thursdays to come and teach us how to play them.

We'd also added tenor recorders to our stock of descants, and more and more teachers were willing to have a go, even if, like me, they couldn't read music. The children handled the tenors well, so why not get a few clarinets too? Or would they prove too difficult for our children? I bought five, found a superb teacher – and before long they too could play Jingle Bells ... a stunningly effective, jazzed-up version.

As the years passed, we added more and more instruments. And then, last September, I realized we had all the components for a full orchestra, and a deputy head with the skills to put it all together. We practised like mad before school on Thursdays, and for a while I wondered if it had been such a good idea. And then, one morning just before Christmas, everything seemed to gel. Every child sensed that something magical had happened and that they'd played together beautifully.

These days, the reputation of our school orchestra is spreading quickly, but the excitement of their first real 'gig' this Summer, opening the Southwark deputy heads' conference at a swanky seaside hotel, was a highlight.

'I'll never forget today', whispered a little violinist happily on the coach going home. 'Neither will I, Chloe', I said. 'Neither will I.'

Sixty-one
Oh, go on Miss, just a sip

The weather is hot, and some of my younger staff felt that children needed to have greater access to drinking water during the day, to stop them becoming dehydrated. Could the children bring in water bottles to sip from, as they struggled with the rigours of long division?

In vain I mentioned that I'd been drinking water from the staffroom tap for the last twenty-odd years, and provided there weren't more than two dead pigeons in the water tank it usually tasted pretty good. But the staff assured me that the children's work was bound to improve with a regular intake of water, and since we have the distinction of being a 'healthy school', with an abundance of fruit, good lunches and lots of exercise, I agreed to give it a shot.

The first sign of trouble came when children misinterpreted my Assembly chat about the bottles they could bring. In came an amazing assortment, ranging from the tiny to the two-gallon supersized, often hauled up the stairs by doting mothers who didn't want their offspring to miss out on this new school feature. Eventually, we ruled that only a half-litre see-through plastic bottle was acceptable, and after some initial skirmishes, children kept to this agreed size.

What they didn't keep to was the rule about the contents of the bottle. Soon, liquids of various shades began to appear at classrooms doors, held by mothers with a ready excuse. 'Michelle doesn't like water very much. It makes her throw up, you see, so I've diluted her strawberry-blueberry-bilberry drinks a bit. I'm sure you won't mind if she has a sip of that instead. And I've made it a bit fizzy for her. She just won't drink it otherwise . . .'

Another Assembly, and another explanation about how good old see-through, non-coloured, plain uncarbonated water is the thing your body loves most. Stick to drinking that, I said, and you're bound to grow up as brainy, talented and energetic as your hunky headteacher. They laughed, and for a week or two things seemed to be going well.

Until they discovered that certain types of bottle are wicked weapons for soaking each other in the playground at lunchtimes.

Fill 'em up from the drinking fountains, enlarge the hole in the top, and with a bit of luck and a steady hand you can 'accidentally' drench all your mates from ten metres away.

There's even more fun to be had while standing at the fountain filling your bottle. Position a thumb carefully over the fountain spout and an entire class can be sprayed as they line up. More rules were formed: bottles had to be left in classrooms at all times, and were only to be used for drinking from, not as miniature water cannon.

At the next staff meeting, water stayed high on the agenda. When, exactly, were the children allowed to reach for their bottles? Was it acceptable to leap up in the middle of PHSE and take a hefty swig? Should the bottles be kept on desks or at the side of the room? Should they carry names, because Ephram had already swigged from Zainab's bottle by accident and almost started a war. And what were we going to do about trips to the toilet, which had increased a million-fold and were seriously interrupting lessons?

Eventually, even the ardent supporters amongst the staff were becoming fed up with the constant interruptions. New playground fountains are being fitted after the summer holidays, and already the number of classroom bottles is decreasing. Furthermore, we haven't noticed the slightest deterioration in the children's work.

And then, just as everything was settling down again, six huge cardboard boxes were delivered to school. A free present from the Healthy Schools scheme. Four hundred plastic bottles of water ...

Sixty-two
Some of our children are missing

We run a Summer Camp at half term, and this year 30 children set off for an activity-filled three days at a Scouts centre in Essex.

Because we've been organizing these camping trips for years, the whole thing usually passes uneventfully. Perhaps I should have been a little suspicious when the coach arrived to pick up the children and the driver wouldn't let anybody on because he was still owed 12 minutes of his break. But after this initial hitch, off they went, had a marvellous time exploring, climbing and canoeing, and they were looking forward to seeing their parents on Friday afternoon, happy but worn out from all the excitement.

At two o'clock, Secretary Sandra came into the school hall, where I was rehearsing the summer musical. 'We might have a problem', she said. 'I've been ringing the coach firm since nine this morning to check they'll be on time, and there's no answer. And Kathy has rung to say the coach hasn't turned up at the camp. It was due over an hour ago.'

I felt an icy hand grip my stomach. We hadn't used this firm before. What if they'd gone bankrupt and simply abandoned their jobs? In two hours, the parents would be coming to collect their children. I suggested Sandra try some other firms. There were plenty locally and some would have a spare coach, wouldn't they? No, she'd already tried that, and unfortunately they hadn't.

What to do? I phoned the teacher in charge, and said the best thing would be to leave the luggage at the camp and come back by train. We could have the luggage collected the following week, and getting the children home was my priority. Five minutes later, the teacher was back on the phone; the camp refused to hold the luggage and the children would have to take it on the train. I was astonished. When I was a Scout, the idea had been to be as helpful as possible to people.

Then I had a thought. One of my part-time teachers owned a van. I could travel with him and we could collect the luggage in that. He agreed to come in, and I rushed home for my trusty sat nav, as even in the Scouts I invariably got maps upside down and ended up travelling backwards. When I returned to school, parents were already gathering, and a number were grumbling, wondering why we hadn't phoned them to say the children would be late. How I love parents when there's a crisis!

Meanwhile, there had been developments. The coach had now arrived at the camp, well over two hours late. The driver had been stuck in traffic, but neither he nor the firm had bothered to let us know. Worse, after telephoning every hire firm in a 50-mile radius of the centre, one of the teachers at the camp had managed to secure two mini buses and they were now on their way to the camp at a cost of £600, paid on his credit card.

Although they hadn't gone very far when the coach arrived, the company refused to reimburse his card, until they realized they were dealing with a hot, tired and very angry teacher who'd been trying to contain 35 frustrated children on a narrow piece of parched ground at the pick-up point. Grumbling, they eventually agreed to bring the charge down to £150.

By half past six the children were safely back at school, most had been collected by their parents, and one teacher remained to look after the stragglers. I felt an intense sense of relief. Fortunately, it had all ended well.

Harold Wilson once said that a week is a long time in politics. It's a lot longer in education.

Sixty-three
Sadness and celebration

It's the end of the summer term, and time for the Year 6 leavers' concert.

Music and drama have always been high priorities at our school, and the idea of a leavers' concert started years ago, when a handful of children thought it might be nice to entertain the rest of the school with a few songs, a couple of dances, and a sketch lampooning the staff – which, since they were leaving that day, they knew they weren't going to be told off for.

And then, like Topsy, the event just seemed to grow each year. As our standards of music and performance climbed higher, so did the quality of the leavers' concert. This year, preparations began early, as last year's cohort had set a high standard, and, as usual, parents of Year 6 children were invited to come along too. Many always do, partly because their children talk excitedly about the concert, but also because they are grateful and want to share their children's last moments at the school.

The entire school crowds into the hall which we've made into our little theatre, the lights on the stage fire up, and the chattering dies down to an expectant whisper. As the show begins, I realize just how accomplished our children have become during their seven years with us. With the help of their teachers, they have designed an enormously varied programme ... Indian dancing, comedy wrestling that keeps the Infants in fits of laughter, African songs and dances, genuinely amusing sketches, solo and group singing of current songs that are tunefully and skilfully performed. And there are moments of great unintentional humour, too. When Michael has to introduce the next act with only two words, he forgets one of them.

The staffroom sketch is, as usual, greeted with hoots of laughter and appreciation. But this one is cleverer than before. How well these children know us, I think to myself. Our mannerisms, our personalities – but this year it all seems to be done with greater affection ... and a little sadness. They know we are fond of them, and they like us, too. The sketch ends with a child impersonating a recently retired member of staff, cartwheeling across the stage and shouting 'I'm free! Oh God, at last I'm free!'

Then, back to the music, and most moving of all, the five girls we now call our Camberwell Beauties. One of our teachers had heard them singing together in the playground two years earlier, inventing harmonies to a song we'd taught them in choir. She took time out of her lunch hour to work with them, finding songs that would suit their voices. When she left, other teachers took over, pushing the boundaries and not letting them get away with merely regurgitating currently fashionable pop songs. And now, watching this concert, I am hearing a stunningly beautiful rendition of 'Down To The River To Pray', each one of the five singing a different harmony. How sad that they are leaving us today.

And then the children line up on stage for their finale. 'I want to be ... a footballer', says Michael, the first in the row. 'I want to be ... a designer', says Rachel. And so on, round the circle, each child voicing hopes and dreams for the future. A few will live their dreams. Many won't. But for this brief moment in time, the world is theirs.

The concert ends, the rest of the school goes out to play, and Year 6 climbs down from the stage. The children are quiet and subdued. The moment has arrived, and they are about to leave us. Many, despite themselves, are in tears, and I hug each one. They are my children, I will miss them, and I am reminded, once again, how privileged we are to be teachers.

Sixty-four
September? Not a month I mind

On the last Saturday of term, when I popped into the DVD shop to rent a film, the owner smiled and said 'Almost the end of term then. You must be looking forward to it.' Then on to the hairdresser, who said 'Only a few days now. I bet you can't wait ...'

Funny how everyone says the same thing to a teacher. There's an assumption that you're crawling towards the summer holiday break on your hands and knees.

In fact, I'm never in that much of a hurry for term to end. Yes, the holidays are thoroughly enjoyable, but then, so is school, and I count myself fortunate in working with 350 fascinating little human beings. In my entire career, I've never had a day when I haven't felt like going to work.

But that's not to say a school year doesn't have its peaks and troughs, and when I look back, this one has been no exception. We've had our usual quota of irritating people, like the auditor from Human Resources who found my room an annoying place because funny little things called children kept coming in and showing me their work. Or the photocopier salesmen who ring up every five minutes telling you that they can offer the school the bargain of the century, provided you'll sign up for a mere five years.

Then Secretary Sandra was called for jury service, and, since she is so skilful and efficient that I don't need to employ any other admin staff, this was a real worry. Sandra has a photographic memory, and can retain all those little details I would instantly forget, such as Mrs Andrews paying half of Andrea's dinner money for next month because she hasn't got the whole lot just yet and could Sandra please remember that it includes money for film club and fruit but not book club because she'll send that separately. My biggest worry was that Sandra's case would turn out to be the crime of the century and she'd be away for the rest of the term.

February brought huge snow drifts, frozen pipes and problems with teachers moving their cars onto the main road, let alone getting to school. And when spring arrived, we received a massive water bill and, on investigation, found the water meter needle spinning around like a whirling dervish. There was obviously a leak underneath the playground. Somewhere.

And every year something happens which causes me to say 'Well, this is a first.' This year was true to form. We spent several weeks trying to track down the phantom urinator who left little yellow puddles on the staircases, in the corridors and, on one occasion, in a sink. We didn't find him … and then it stopped as suddenly as it had started.

But the year's peaks vastly outweighed the troughs. Our orchestra and jazz group combining to learn a spirited version of 'Rock Around The Clock'. The constant enthusiasm of my staff, and their real desire that every child in their charge should achieve as much as they were able. The amazingly inventive models produced in our technology competition. The pleasures of Poetry Week. The children creating their own brilliantly colourful costumes, masks and head-dresses for our spectacular Carnival. Our Summer Musical in which, on the hottest of July evenings, we packed our hall with excited parents and children. The enjoyment of helping train a future leader and feeling instinctively that he will eventually make an excellent headteacher. And letters from some of the secondary schools we feed, telling us that our ex-pupils are a pleasure to teach.

So, yes, I'll enjoy my summer holiday. I'll read a lot. I'll write, I'll go to the cinema. I'll listen to plenty of music and play my guitar and banjo. I'll go to the seaside, visit places, and have lots of time to enjoy my wife's company. But when September comes around, I shan't be sorry.

Because I'll be back doing the thing I love most.

August

School closed for the summer holiday

Index